WJEC EDUQAS GCSE WORKBOOK

Revise English Language

Michelle Doran

Natalie Simpson

Julie Swain

Consultant:
Barry Childs

OXFORD
UNIVERSITY PRESS

OXFORD
UNIVERSITY PRESS

Great Clarendon Street, Oxford, OX2 6DP, United Kingdom

Oxford University Press is a department of the University of Oxford.

It furthers the University's objective of excellence in research, scholarship, and education by publishing worldwide. Oxford is a registered trade mark of Oxford University Press in the UK and in certain other countries

© Oxford University Press 2016

First published in 2016

British Library Cataloguing in Publication Data

Data available

ISBN 978-019-835921-0

10 9 8 7 6 5 4

Printed in India by Multivista Global Pvt. Ltd

Acknowledgements

The authors and publisher are grateful for permission to reprint extracts from the following copyright material:

Kate Atkinson: *Behind the Scenes at the Museum* (Black Swan, 1996), copyright © Kate Atkinson 1995, reprinted by permission of The Random House Group Ltd.

Margaret Atwood: 'Hurricane Hazel' in Bluebeard's Egg and Other Stories (Cape, 1987), copyright © O W Toad Ltd 1983, 1987, reprinted by permission of The Random House Group Ltd.

Andrew Baker: 'Chocolate: 10 Health reasons you should eat more of it', The Telegraph, 22 Feb 2016, copyright © Telegraph Media Group Ltd 2016, reprinted by permission of Telegraph Media Group.

Toni Cade Bambara: 'Raymond's Run', copyright © Toni Cade Bambara 1971, from Gorilla, My Love (Vintage 1981), reprinted by permission of Random House, an imprint and division of Penguin Random House LLC. All rights reserved.

Fran Bardsley: 'Vandalised playgrounds swing back into action', Oxford Mail, 27 June 2011, reprinted by permission of the Oxford Mail, Newsquest Media Group Ltd.

Bill Bryson: *The Complete Notes* (Doubleday, 2000), copyright © Bill Bryson 2000, reprinted by permission of The Random House Group Ltd.

Roald Dahl: 'Galloping Foxley' from *Someone Like You* (Penguin, 2012), copyright © Roald Dahl 1954, reprinted by permission of David Higham Associates.

Sebastian Faulks: *Birdsong* (Vintage, 2014), copyright © Sebastian Faulks 1993, reprinted by permission of The Random House Group Ltd.

Neil Gaiman: *Stardust* (Headline, 2005), copyright © Neil Gaiman 2005, reprinted by permission of Headline Publishing, Hachette UK.

Arthur Golden: *Memoirs of a Geisha* (Chatto & Windus, 1997), copyright © Arthur Golden 1997, reprinted by permission of The Random House Group Ltd.

Emily Hodson: 'Adam Richman's Fast Food Filth: Man v Food's dangerous message', on MoonProject.co.uk, 6 Jan 2013, reprinted by permission of MoonProject.

India Knight: 'Stop swearing at the sky and join me for a snow snuggle', The Sunday Times, 20 Jan 2013, copyright © India Knight/ News UK and Ireland Ltd 2013, reprinted by permission of News Syndication.

Alexander McCall Smith: *Portuguese Irregular Verbs* (Polygon, 2003), copyright © Alexander McCall Smith 2003, reprinted by permission of David Higham Associates.

Ian McEwan: *Enduring Love* (Cape, 1997), copyright © Ian McEwan 1997, reprinted by permission of The Random House Group Ltd.

Ruth Margolis: 'Target is abolishing boy/girl toy labels' The Week, 13 Aug 2015, reprinted by permission of The Week Publications, Inc.

George R R Martin: *A Game of Thrones* (Harper Voyager, 2014), copyright © George R R Martin 2014, reprinted by permission of HarperCollins Publishers Ltd.

Rohinton Mistry: *A Fine Balance* (Faber, 2006), copyright © Rohinton Mistry 1995, reprinted by permission of Faber & Faber Ltd.

Maseeh Rahman: 'India's slumdog census reveals poor condiions for one of six urban dwellers', theguardian.com, 22 March 2013, copyright © Guardian News & Media 2013, 2016, reprinted by permission of Guardian News & Media Ltd.

Louis Sachar: *Holes* (Bloomsbury, 2015), copyright © Louis Sachar 2015, reprinted by permission of Bloomsbury Publishing Plc.

Amy Tan: *The Hundred Secret Senses* (Flamingo, 1995/Penguin, 2010), copyright © Amy Tan 1995, reprinted by permission of HarperCollins Publishers Ltd and Abner Stein on behalf of the author.

Janice Turner: 'CCTV Britain, the world's most paranoid nation', The Times, 13 July 2013, copyright © Janice Turner/ News UK and Ireland Ltd 2013, reprinted by permission of News Syndication.

Although we have made every effort to trace and contact all copyright holders before publication this has not been possible in all cases. If notified, the publisher will rectify any errors or omissions at the earliest opportunity.

The publisher and authors would like the thank the following for permission to use photographs and other copyright material:

COVER: © Jack Affleck / Getty Images

p98: The National Archives; **p103:** British Library.

Contents

Introduction — 4

WJEC Eduqas English Language
specification overview — 4

How this workbook is structured — 5

What are the main features within
this workbook? — 5

Component 1 Section A: Reading — 6
Summary of Component 1
Section A: Reading — 6
Unit 1: Assessment Objective 1 — 7
   1 Location of explicit details — 7
   2 Location and interpretation
     of implicit details — 10
Unit 2: Assessment Objective 2 — 17
   3 How writers use language — 17
   4 How writers use structure — 21
   5 How writers create effect — 23
   6 How writers influence their readers — 25
Unit 3: Assessment Objective 4 — 28
   7 Bringing the writer's craft together — 28
   8 Personal and critical evaluation — 34

Component 1 Section B: Writing — 41
Summary of Component 1
Section B: Writing — 41
   1 Planning to write — 42
   2 Openings — 45
   3 Organizing and structuring — 49
   4 Developing the narrative: settings — 55
   5 Developing the narrative: characters — 60
   6 Effective endings — 65

Component 2 Section A: Reading — 67
Summary of Component 2
Section A: Reading — 67
Unit 1: Assessment Objective 1 — 68
   1 Location of explicit details — 68
   2 Location and interpretation
     of implicit details — 73
   3 Combining information from
     two texts — 80
Unit 2: Assessment Objective 2 — 84
   4 How writers use language — 84
Unit 3: Assessment Objective 3 — 90
   5 Comparing information and ideas
     from two texts — 90
   6 Comparing how the writers
     get across their views — 94
   7 Comparing information and how
     writers get across their views — 97
Unit 4: Assessment Objective 4 — 103
   8 Evaluating texts critically with
     supporting textual detail — 103

Component 2 Section B: Writing — 112
Summary of Component 2
Section B: Writing — 112
   1 Formal letters — 113
   2 Writing an informal letter or email — 121
   3 Writing speeches/talks — 127
   4 Writing an article — 134
   5 Reports — 141
   6 Writing a review — 147

Sample exam papers — 152
Sample Component 1 Section A — 152
Sample Component 1 Section B — 155
Sample Component 2 Section A — 156
Sample Component 2 Section B — 159

Glossary — 160

WJEC Eduqas GCSE English Language specification overview

The exam papers

The grade you receive at the end of your WJEC Eduqas GCSE English Language course is entirely based on your performance in two exam papers. The following table provides a summary of these two papers.

Exam paper	Reading and Writing questions	Assessment Objectives	Timing	Marks (and % of GCSE)
Component 1: 20th-century Literature Reading Study and Creative Prose Writing	Section A Reading: This section includes structured questions based on your reading of an unseen extract from one 20th-century literary prose text (about 60-100 lines).	AO1 AO2 AO4	1 hour 45 minutes	Reading: 40 marks (20% of GCSE) Writing: 40 marks (20% of GCSE) Component 1 total: 80 marks (40% of GCSE)
	Section B Writing: This section tests creative prose writing through one 40-mark task. You will be offered a choice of four titles giving opportunities for writing to describe and narrate, and imaginative and creative use of language. This response should be a narrative / recount. If you write purely descriptively, or use a form other than that specified, such as poetry or drama, you will not be able to access the full marks available.	AO5 AO6		
Component 2: 19th- and 21st- century Non-fiction Reading Study and Transactional/ Persuasive writing	Section A Reading: This section includes structured questions based on your reading of two high-quality unseen non-fiction texts (about 900-1200 words in total), one from the 19th century, the other from the 21st century. Non-fiction texts may include, but will not be limited to: letters, extracts from autobiographies or biographies, diaries, reports, articles and digital and multi-modal texts of various kinds from newspapers and magazines, and the internet.	AO1 AO2 AO3 AO4	2 hours	Reading: 40 marks (30% of GCSE) Writing: 40 marks (30% of GCSE) Component 1 total: 80 marks (60% of GCSE)
	Section B Writing: This section will test transactional, persuasive and/or discursive writing through two equally weighted compulsory tasks (20 marks each). Across the two tasks you will be offered opportunities to write for a range of audiences and purposes, adapting style to form and to real-life contexts in, for example, letters, articles, reviews, speeches, etc.	AO5 AO6		

To access sample papers and sample mark schemes for the specification, visit:
http://www.eduqas.co.uk/qualifications/english-language/gcse/

How this workbook is structured

Reading

The Reading sections of this workbook take you through the requirements of each assessment objective for Section A for each of the two exam papers. As well as guidance and activities, you will also find extracts of sample student responses and examiner commentaries. There are spaces to write your answers into throughout the workbook.

Writing

The Writing sections of this workbook focus on preparing you for the types of writing you will face in Section B of each of the two exam papers. You will also find a range of strategies to help you when approaching the writing tasks as well as practice opportunities.

Sample exam papers

The workbook concludes with two full sample exam papers, one for Component 1 and one for Component 2.

What are the main features within this workbook?

Activities and texts

To help you practise your reading responses, you will find activities throughout this workbook all linked to the types of questions you will face in your exams. The source texts also reflect the types of texts you will be reading and responding to in your exams.

Tips and Key terms

These features help support your understanding of key terms, concepts and more difficult words within a source text or exam question. These therefore enable you to concentrate fully on developing your exam response skills.

Progress check

You will find regular formative assessments in the form of Progress checks. These enable you to establish how confident you feel about what you have been learning and help you to identify areas for further practice.

Component 1 Section A: Reading

Summary of Component 1 Section A: Reading

Component 1: Whole paper
• 40% of total marks for GCSE English Language
• Assessment length: 1 hour 45 minutes
• Section A – Reading
• Section B – Writing

Section A
• Half marks for Paper (20% of total grade)
• Short and long answers
• Time required: 1 hour (10 minutes reading/50 minutes answering questions)

Section A of Component 1 will test you on your ability to read and understand a piece of 20th-century literary prose writing. This means that you will be assessed on your understanding of an extract of narrative fiction (a story) that was published between 1900 and 1999.

Section A is worth half of the marks available for Component 1 and will be marked out of a total of 40 marks. You will be expected to answer a series of structured questions that will test your knowledge of the writer's meaning and how they have established that meaning.

Assessment Objectives

Section A (Reading) of the Component 1 exam will test your abilities in the following assessment objectives (AOs):

AO1	Identify and interpret explicit and implicit information and ideas. Select and synthesize evidence from different texts.
AO2	Explain, comment on and analyse how writers use language and structure to achieve effects and influence readers, using relevant subject terminology to support their views.
AO4	Evaluate texts critically and support this with appropriate textual references.

Unit 1: Assessment Objective 1

1 Location of explicit details

Learning focus:

- Considering helpful ways to approach the reading of a fictional text
- Revising how to identify **explicit** information and ideas
- Exploring ways to present the information you have located

This section will guide you through the skills you will need to approach a Reading text in your Component 1 exam. You will complete a number of activities that will help you revise how to locate explicit information and ideas within a text. You will then practise answering this type of question yourself.

Activity 1

a. Read the following information:

It is important that you track through a text carefully and **chronologically** when answering an exam question. This means that you should read the text carefully and sentence by sentence. This is important because:

- addressing the text in the order that it is written will provide structure and clarity to your answer
- sometimes details that you read first will help you to understand and make sense of information that is presented later.

b. In your own words, write three bullet points for your revision notes that will help you to remember why tracking the text is important.

- --

- --

- --

Activity 2

a. Read the extract carefully.

Holes by Louis Sachar

Stanley Yelnats was the only passenger on the bus, not counting the driver or the guard. The guard sat next to the driver with his seat turned around facing Stanley. A rifle lay across his lap.

Stanley was sitting about ten rows back, handcuffed to his armrest. His backpack lay on the seat next to him. It contained his toothbrush, toothpaste, and a box of stationery his mother had given him. He'd promised to write to her at least once a week.

Activity 2 continued

He looked out of the window, although there wasn't much to see – mostly fields of hay and cotton. He was on a long bus ride to nowhere. The bus wasn't air-conditioned, and the hot, heavy air was almost as stifling as the handcuffs.

Stanley and his parents had tried to pretend that he was just going away to camp for a while, just like rich kids do. When Stanley was younger he used to play with stuffed animals, and pretend the animals were at camp. Camp Fun and Games he called it. Sometimes he'd have them play soccer with a marble. Other times they'd run an obstacle course, or go bungee jumping off a table, tied to broken rubber bands. Now Stanley tried to pretend he was going to Camp Fun and Games. Maybe he'd make some friends, he thought. At least he'd get to swim in the lake.

He didn't have any friends at home. He was overweight and the kids at his middle school often teased him about his size. Even his teachers sometimes made cruel comments without realizing it.

b. Now read the exam-style question below.

> List five details you learn about Stanley Yelnats. **[5]**

c. Using a highlighter pen, re-read the extract and highlight any evidence that provides you with information about Stanley Yelnats.

Activity 3

Using your highlighted evidence, write down as many points as you can about Stanley. Try to present them in the order in which they come in the text.

_____

_____

_____

_____

_____

Tips

• Re-read the question to remind you of what you are being asked to do. Highlight or underline key words that make it clear what you have to do.

• Be specific when selecting evidence – only highlight the relevant words or phrases.

Activity 4

a. Now look at the following sample answer and tick any points that this student got right.

1. Stanley is overweight and gets teased a lot by other kids. ☐
2. Stanley likes going to camp and swimming in the lake. ☐
3. Stanley is poor and can only play football with a marble. ☐

Activity 4 continued

    4. Stanley is on a bus. ☐

    5. Stanley had promised to write to his mum. ☐

b. Write a comment to explain to the student where the answer is wrong. What advice would you offer this student to improve their answer?

_____

_____

_____

Activity 5

a. Read the extract below carefully.

Stardust by Neil Gaiman

Dunstan Thorn was eighteen, and he was not a romantic.

He had nut-brown hair, and nut-brown eyes, and nut-brown freckles. He was middling tall, and slow of speech. He had an easy smile, which illuminated his face from within, and he dreamed, when he daydreamed in his father's meadow, of leaving the village of Wall and all its unpredictable charm, and going to London, or Edinburgh, or Dublin, or some great town where nothing was dependent on which way the wind was blowing. He worked on his father's farm and owned nothing save a small cottage in a far field given to him by his parents.

Visitors were coming to Wall that April for the fair, and Dunstan resented them. Mr Bromios's inn, the *Seventh Magpie*, normally a warren of empty rooms, had filled a week earlier, and now the strangers had begun to take rooms in the farms and private houses, paying for their lodgings with strange coins, with herbs and spices, and even with gemstones.

b. Complete the following table by answering the questions and providing evidence to support your answers.

Question	Answer/Evidence
How old is Dunstan Thorn?	
What do you find out about Dunstan's appearance?	
What do you find out about Dunstan's hopes for the future?	
Where does Dunstan work?	
How does Dunstan feel about the visitors to Wall?	
What do we find out about Mr Bromios's inn?	
Where else can visitors stay?	

2 Location and interpretation of implicit details

Learning focus:

- Revising how to identify and **interpret implicit** information and ideas
- Exploring ways to discuss and develop the information you have located

In an exam you may need to work with some of the explicit information you find to show that you understand its full meaning. There will be times when you need to explore the implicit information in a text and the **inferences** that can be made based on that. In answering a question that is testing your ability to locate information, you may draw upon explicit evidence but you may also need to stand back from the text and interpret what your evidence implies or reveals.

Key terms

Interpret: to explain the meaning of something said or written, or of someone's actions.

Implicit: suggested but not directly expressed.

Inference: a conclusion reached on the basis of evidence and reasoning.

Activity 1

a. Read the extract below carefully.

Hurricane Hazel by Margaret Atwood

Buddy was a lot older than I was. He was eighteen, almost nineteen, and he'd quit school long ago to work at a garage. He had his own car, a third-hand Dodge, which he kept spotlessly clean and shining. He smoked and drank beer, though he drank the beer only when he wasn't out with me but was with other boys his own age. He would mention how many bottles he had drunk in an offhand way, as if disclaiming praise.

He made me anxious, because I didn't know how to talk to him. Our phone conversations consisted mainly of pauses and monosyllables, though they went on a long time; which was infuriating to my father, who would walk past me in the hall, snapping his first two fingers together like a pair of scissors, meaning I was to cut it short. But cutting short a conversation with Buddy was like trying to divide water, because Buddy's conversations had no shape [...] I hadn't yet learned any of those stratagems girls were supposed to use on men. I didn't know how to ask leading questions, or how to lie about certain kinds of things, which I was later to call being tactful. So mostly I said nothing, which didn't seem to bother Buddy at all.

I knew enough to realize, however, that it was a bad tactic to appear too smart. But if I had chosen to show off, Buddy might not have minded: he was the kind of boy for whom cleverness was female. Maybe he would have liked a controlled display of it, as if it were a special kind of pie or a piece of well-done embroidery. But I never figured out what Buddy wanted; I never figured out why Buddy was going out with me in the first place. Possibly it was because I was there.

Activity 1 continued

b. Now read and answer the exam-style question below.

What do you learn about Buddy and Hazel and the
relationship between them? [5]

What specific
details/information
can you find?

The information should relate specifically
to Buddy, Hazel and their relationship.

Tip

Before beginning
your answer,
spend a couple of
minutes tracking
through the text
and highlighting key
words or phrases
you will use. It may
be helpful to use
different-coloured
pens for information
relating to Buddy,
Hazel and then their
relationship.

10
minutes

Activity 2

Read the following student answers that have been marked and the commentary from the examiner.

Student answer 1

This is speculative – there is no evidence to support this view.

Simple comment but relevant to the question.

Trying to get to implicit meaning but this is speculative – we can't know that he 'quit school' because he didn't 'care about his education'.

In these lines I learned that Buddy is a lot older than Hazel, as it says 'Buddy was a lot older than I was'. Buddy had 'quit school long ago to work in a garage' – this gives me the impression that Buddy doesn't care about his education. He was a typical teenager. 'He smoked and drank beer', although he only drank beer when he wasn't with Hazel. This suggests he doesn't want to be with her a lot of the time. Their relationship isn't very good because 'she didn't know how to talk to him.' This gives me the impression that she isn't confident with him. She didn't know why he was going out with her as she says 'I never figured out why Buddy was going out with me in the first place.' She said it's possibly because 'I was there'.

Again this is a little vague – a clear point is not being made.

A simple comment – quite vague – needs to be more clearly linked to the evidence.

Examiner comment

This student makes some straightforward comments with reference to the text. There is some attempt to explain the evidence used and some range of points made, but not the demonstration of clear understanding that would gain a higher mark. 4 out of 10 marks.

Activity 2 continued

Student answer 2

> Some appropriate selections made and the candidate tries to develop their explanation of what it tells us about the character.

> The candidate has located a good range of points already in relation to explicit information revealed about Buddy's character.

In these lines, I learned that Buddy is a 'lot older' than Hazel. He was 'eighteen' and had 'quit school' to work in a garage. He 'drank beer' but only when he wasn't out with her, which shows that he understands the age difference and to keep her safe. He made her 'anxious' because she didn't know how to talk to him. Their conversations were mainly 'pauses and monosyllables', which shows that they didn't really know what to say to each other. They were on the phone for a long time, much to her father's annoyance, saying nothing. Buddy's conversations had 'no shape', which suggests he didn't know what to talk about that would interest a girl so much younger than him. As she had not learned 'the stratagems' for dealing with men, such as asking 'leading questions' or telling certain kinds of lies, she mostly said 'nothing' and it didn't bother Buddy at all, which suggests he is easy-going. Buddy thinks 'cleverness is female', which suggests he isn't very smart and wants his girlfriend to be clever. Hazel never knew what Buddy 'really wanted', which suggests that it isn't an equal relationship and that they aren't really close. She thinks he chose her because she 'was there', which suggests that they were going out for the sake of it and it was convenient for Buddy.

> The candidate is able to build upon the evidence, keeping in mind the requirement to focus on what we learn about the relationship as well as the characters.

> The candidate constantly focuses on what the evidence suggests, making clear and valid points in relation to it.

Examiner comment

This is a thorough and well-considered answer that tracks through the text and considers a full range of evidence. A number of points are made and these are well-supported with evidence from the text. The candidate is able to draw upon explicit information to make a range of different points, as well as making valid inferences in relation to both characters and their relationship. 10 out of 10 marks.

Activity 3

Review your own answer based on what you have read above. Does your work share similarities with either of the answers above? Look at how the examiner has marked the sample answers and try to do the same with your own answer – add comments to demonstrate where you have done well and where you could improve.

Activity 4

With your own feedback in mind, rewrite your answer.

Activity 5

a. Read the extract below carefully.

A Fine Balance by Rohinton Mistry

Maneck found his compartment. [...] The whistle sounded. [...] He sank into the seat beside his fellow passenger.

The man did not encourage Maneck's efforts at conversation, answering with nods and grunts, or vague hand movements. He was neatly dressed, his hair parted on the left. His shirt pocket bristled with pens and markers in a special clip-on plastic case. [...]

In the evening Maneck offered his neatly dressed neighbour a Gluco biscuit. He whispered thank you. 'You're welcome,' Maneck whispered back, assuming the man had a preference for speaking softly. In return for the biscuit he received a banana. Its skin was blackened in the heat, but he ate it all the same.

The attendant began making the rounds with blankets and sheets, readying the berths for sleep. After he left, the neatly dressed man took a chain and padlock from his bag and shackled his trunk to a bracket under the seat. Leaning towards Maneck's ear, he explained confidentially, 'Because of thieves – they enter the compartments when passengers fall asleep.'

'Oh,' said Maneck, a little perturbed. No one had warned him about this. But maybe the chap was just a nervous type. 'You know, some years ago my mother and I took this same train, and nothing was stolen.'

'Sadly, now the world is much changed.' The man took off his shirt and hung it neatly on a hook by the window. Then he removed the plastic case from the shirt pocket and clipped it to his vest, careful not to snare his chest hair in the formidable spring. Seeing Maneck watching, he whispered with a smile, 'I am very fond of my pens. I don't like separating from them, not even in sleep.'

Activity 5 continued

b. Now read the exam-style question below.

> What do you learn about Maneck's fellow passenger in this section of the text? **[10]**

Make a list of any information or details you learn about Maneck's fellow passenger.

Activity 6

a. Look at the list below of some of the things you could have mentioned about the passenger.

Points about the passenger	Evidence
• He did not encourage Maneck's attempts at conversation. • He was quiet/unwilling to speak. • He was 'neatly dressed'. • He was well-groomed. • He carried pens/markers in a 'special clip-on plastic case' in his shirt pocket. • He was willing to share food with Maneck. • He was softly spoken. • He was cautious and well-prepared. • He seemed knowledgeable about the dangers of travelling. • Maneck wonders if he is a 'nervous type'. • He is careful with his things. • He is not very trusting.	

Support

Some of the details we learn will come from the writer explicitly telling us – for example, we know that the passenger 'did not encourage Maneck's efforts at conversation'.

Some of the details we learn come through our own powers of deduction and reasoning when reading the text – for example, we could deduce that the passenger is a quiet person or unwilling to speak.

Activity 6 continued

b. How many of these points did you make? Do you have any more that you could add to the list?

c. Some of the points use evidence explicitly, but others have inferred meaning from the text. Complete the table with evidence to support those points that are not directly told to you in the text.

Activity 7

a. Read the sample student answer below and the examiner comment that was made.

What do you learn about Maneck's fellow passenger in this section of the text? **[10]**

Student answer

We learn that Maneck's fellow passenger seems quite quiet and is not very friendly at first. We know that he 'did not encourage Maneck's efforts at conversation'. We learn that he is neat and tidy in the way that he is dressed. We are told that he is 'neatly dressed' and 'his hair parted on the left'. We learn that he carries around pens in a 'special clip-on plastic case' in his shirt pocket, which makes it sound like he might really need his pens or be a bit obsessive about them. We learn that the passenger likes to keep his things safe and 'shackled his trunk to a bracket under the seat' before going to sleep. He doesn't seem to trust the other passengers and seems an experienced traveller as he warns of 'thieves' who 'enter the compartment' when passengers fall asleep.

Examiner comment

This answer is careful to keep the focus of the question in mind. The candidate uses short but relevant quotations to effectively support some of the points being made. The candidate includes some explicit detail from the text but also is able to make some inferences that show understanding of what is being revealed about the passenger. There is some information and detail that has been overlooked though, and there was the opportunity to use additional supporting evidence to really develop some points and this was not taken. This answer begins well but it does not have the range of content or development of detail for a mark in the top band. 7 out of 10 marks.

b. Annotate the answer with any improvements that you think would help to improve its mark.

Activity 8

Exchange books with a partner. Read the improvements that your partner has made to the answer. Using a different-coloured pen, write in anything that you think they have missed or see if you can offer further development to any points they have made.

Unit 2: Assessment Objective 2

3 How writers use language

Learning focus:

- Revising how to **analyse** a writer's use of language
- Exploring layers of meaning in writing

Analysing language involves looking at meaning, or the layers of meaning, that have been created in a piece of writing. It involves exploring what the writer did to create that meaning. An expert reader must engage with the content of a text in order to work out how the writer has created meaning.

In your exams you will be expected to use relevant subject terminology to support your views. The key word here is 'relevant', and you should make sure that if you are referring to specific terminology it is done to make clear how a writer creates meaning. Avoid 'feature spotting', such as telling the examiner you have found **alliteration** or a **simile**, unless you are mentioning these details in order to make a clear point about why they are there.

Key terms

Analyse: to examine something methodically and in detail, in order to explain and interpret it.

Alliteration: the same letter or sound at the beginning of a group of words for special effect.

Simile: a figure of speech in which one thing is compared to another using the words 'as' or 'like'.

Activity 1

Answer the following questions in your own words:

a. What is meant by the phrase 'layers of meaning'?

----

b. What will you look at when engaging with 'the content of a text'?

----

c. What does the word 'relevant' mean?

----

d. Why should you avoid 'feature spotting'?

Activity 2

a. Earlier in this workbook you encountered the phrase 'tracking through the text'. Write down an explanation of what this means.

----

b. Explain why it might be important to 'track' through the text when answering a question about analysing language.

Activity 3

a. Read the extract below carefully.

A Game of Thrones by George R. R. Martin

The sounds of music and song spilled through the open windows behind him. They were the last things Jon wanted to hear. He wiped away his tears on the sleeve of his shirt, furious that he had let them fall, and turned to go.

"Boy," a voice called out to him. Jon turned.

Tyrion Lannister was sitting on the ledge above the door to the Great Hall, looking for all the world like a gargoyle. The dwarf grinned down at him. "Is that animal a wolf?"

"A direwolf," Jon said. "His name is Ghost." He stared up at the little man, his disappointment suddenly forgotten. "What are you doing up there? Why aren't you at the feast?"

"Too hot, too noisy, and I'd drunk too much wine," the dwarf told him. "I learned long ago that it is considered rude to vomit on your brother. Might I have a closer look at your wolf?"

Jon hesitated, then nodded slowly. "Can you climb down, or shall I bring a ladder?"

"Oh, bleed that," the little man said. He pushed himself off the ledge into empty air. Jon gasped, then watched in awe as Tyrion Lannister spun around in a tight ball, landed lightly on his hands, then vaulted backwards onto his legs.

b. Now read the exam-style question below.

> What impressions do you get of Tyrion Lannister in this extract?
>
> You should write about:
>
> - your impressions of Tyrion as he is presented here
> - how the writer has created these impressions   **[10]**

Activity 3 continued

c. Complete the following table, paying careful attention to the language (words/phrases/ images) the writer uses and how this creates meaning. Keep in mind that the same evidence may contribute to creating more than one impression.

Impressions	How is this impression created? What evidence can you use to prove it?
He is commanding.	His first word is 'Boy', which suggests he is older than Jon. This establishes his seniority and he uses it as a one-word command for Jon's attention.
He is ugly.	He looked 'for all the world like a gargoyle', which suggests that his figure is bent and his face ugly to the point of being frightening.

Activity 4

The answer below has some weaknesses and the student has not analysed the language sufficiently to score a high mark. The examiner has highlighted areas where the student could have examined the writer's use of language in more detail. Complete the boxes to suggest how this could be improved.

This isn't quite right. He had actually 'learned long ago that it is considered rude to vomit on your brother' which suggests he left because...

This is valid but a little vague...

The writer gives the impression that Tyrion Lannister is a dwarf and he is not attractive. He is a heavy drinker and was sick on his brother. It is dangerous for him to be so high up if he has had too much to drink and we think he will probably hurt himself. He seems quite polite to Jon and asks to look at his wolf. We are told that Tyrion 'spun' and 'vaulted' to get off the roof. This makes me think he is quite fit.

This is true but a little vague – it would be better linked to...

This is no more than speculation – there is no evidence to suggest he...

These impressions are valid but quite understated given the evidence that is available to analyse. The candidate could have said...

Activity 5

10 minutes

Now answer the question from page 18 yourself, using the lines below:

Progress check

Look back over what you have written and mark your work in the following ways:

a. Highlight three parts of your answer where you think you have analysed what the writer did to create meaning.

b. In a different colour, highlight one area that could still be improved by further explanation or perhaps by investigating alternative meanings. Using the lines below, jot down what you would do to further improve this.

----

4 How writers use structure

Learning focus:

- Revising the meaning of structure
- Exploring the way a writer uses structure in their writing

In many exam questions that ask you to look at how a writer creates meaning, it may be necessary to comment on the way a writer structures their work. This means the way a piece of writing is organized. A writer deliberately organizes their writing to create meaning and effect.

Activity 1

Write down a definition that will help you remember what structure is.

Activity 2

Read the extract on the next page carefully. Using the comments below as a starting point, annotate the extract (highlighting key evidence at the same time) to show how its structure helps to create meaning.

The writer emphasizes the noise going on for a long time.
Sentence openings are often used to chart the time.
When the order comes there is immediate action.
The unusual silence is emphasized through the sentencing, then by the absence of noise, then by repetition.
The use of dialogue enables the writer to show the immediate feelings of the soldiers.
The confused nature and instinctive reactions of Jack are emphasized by the sentencing...
The concluding sentence of the paragraph emphasizes the reality of the situation.
Jack's quietness is set against the noise to emphasize the contrast.
The writer uses the passing of time to structure the work.
The writer uses the structure to emphasize Frank's fears and how much he thinks about them.
The narrative progresses in a linear way; this means...
Positioning the phrase 'It was death,' at the start of the sentence emphasizes...
The pace deliberately slows to build to the inevitable ending.
The structure emphasizes the wait that the soldiers have and the things they do to pass the time.

Activity 2 continued

Behind the Scenes at the Museum by Kate Atkinson

Frank thought it was probably the noise that got to Jack in the end. For three days and three nights the barrage never stopped and as the guns seemed to get louder, so Jack seemed to get quieter and quieter, although he didn't go mad with it like some chaps, he was just too quiet. Funnily enough, the noise didn't bother Frank so much anymore, he thought it was because he'd got used to the constant booming of the howitzers although in fact he'd gone deaf in his right ear.

It wasn't the noise that bothered Frank anyway – it was death, or rather, how he was going to die, that worried him. There was no doubt he was going to die; after all, he'd been out here nearly two years and the odds were piled high against him by now. Frank had begun to pray his way through the war. He no longer prayed that he wouldn't die, he just prayed he would see it coming. He was terrified of dying without any warning and prayed that he might at least see the mortar that was coming for him so he would have time to prepare himself. Or anticipate in some magical way the sniper's bullet that would take his brain out before his body even knew about it. And please God, he begged, don't let me be gassed. Only a week ago nearly a whole battalion in a trench that ran parallel to this one, a Pals' battalion from a factory in Nottingham, had been taken by a low-level tide of gas that rolled quietly along towards them and took them before they realized what was happening. Now they were all quietly drowning to death in some field-hospital.

The night before the attack nobody could sleep. At four in the morning, when it was already light Frank and Jack lolled against the sandbagged wall of the trench while Frank rolled a cigarette for each of them and one for Alf Simmonds who was ducked down on the firing-step above them on sentry duty. Then Jack sucked on his spindly roll-up and, without looking at Frank, said, 'I'm not going,' and Frank said, 'Not going where?' so that Jack laughed and pointed in the direction of No Man's Land and said 'There, of course – I'm not going there.'

Alf Simmonds laughed as well and said, 'Don't blame you lad,' because he thought it was a joke, but Frank felt sick because he knew it wasn't.

It was silent before the order came. The guns had stopped and there was no laughing or joking or anything, just the silence of waiting. Frank watched the clouds pass over in the blue sky above, little puffs of white that were floating above No Man's Land as if it was any other bit of countryside and not the place where he was going to die very shortly. [...]

When the order came to go over the top it was more like a relief than anything and everyone scrambled up the ladders and over the parapet until there were only three of them left – Frank, Jack and the new lieutenant. [...] the new lieutenant started screaming at them and waving his gun around, saying he was going to shoot them if they didn't go over [...] Then Jack said, 'You don't have to do that, sir, we're going,' and he half-dragged Frank over the top, and before they were even over the parapet Jack was yelling 'Run!' at him, which Frank did, because now he was more frightened of being shot in the back by the new lieutenant's rifle than he was of being blown up by the enemy.

5 How writers create effect

Learning focus:

- Exploring the ways in which a writer creates effect
- Thinking about what an 'effect' is

A writer creates effects by creating impressions in the mind of the reader. The writer may tell us things, deliberately not tell us things or try to influence us through the suggestions they make. To comment on how a writer creates effects, you need to look at the way they deliberately use words and literary devices to create **impressions**.

Key terms

Impression: effect produced on the mind, ideas.

Metaphor: a figure of speech in which a word or phrase is used to describe an object or action without using 'as' or 'like'.

Activity 1

Feature-spotting without comment or explanation will not get you any additional marks – and it can lose you the opportunity to gain further marks by distracting you. However, correctly identifying and commenting on why the use of a particular device is effective can be helpful. Look at the following list of literary devices and terminology. Do you know what they are and how they are used? Complete the table.

Device	Definition	Example	Purpose
Simile	A comparison of two things using the words 'like' or 'as'	The cat was *as black as soot*	
Metaphor			
Personification			
Alliteration			
Assonance			
Irony			
Sarcasm			
Tone			
Cliché			
Hyperbole			
Onomatopoeia			

Activity 2

a. Read the extract below carefully.

> *The Hundred Secret Senses* by Amy Tan
> Here the narrator is just about to meet her older Chinese step-sister for the first time...
>
> I was nearly six by the time Kwan came to this country. We were waiting for her at the customs area of San Francisco Airport. [...] My mother was nervous and excited, talking non-stop: 'Now listen, kids, she'll probably be shy, so don't jump all over her... And she'll be skinny as a beanpole, so I don't want any of you making fun of her...'
>
> When the customs official finally escorted Kwan into the lobby where we were waiting Aunt Betty pointed and said, 'That's her. I'm telling you that's her.' Mom was shaking her head. This person looked like a strange old lady, short and chubby, not exactly the starving waif Mom pictured or the glamorous teenage sister I had in mind. She was dressed in drab gray pyjamas, and her broad brown face was flanked by two thick braids.
>
> Kwan was anything but shy. She dropped her bag, fluttered her arms, and bellowed, 'Hall-oo! Hall-oo!' Still hooting and laughing, she jumped and squealed the way our new dog did whenever we let him out of the garage. This total stranger tumbled into Mom's arms, then Daddy Bob's. She grabbed Kevin and Tommy by the shoulders and shook them. When she saw me, she grew quiet, squatted on the lobby floor, and held out her arms. I tugged on my mother's skirt. 'Is *that* my big sister?'

b. Now record your impressions of Kwan in the table below.

Impressions of Kwan	
Evidence	Effect
'This person looked like a strange old lady, short and chubby...'	The writer uses a simile to compare Kwan to an old lady to convey her small size. We get the sense that she is unusual in appearance through the word 'strange' and perhaps that she looks old before her time.
'... not exactly the starving waif Mom pictured'	Understatement – the writer contrasts the expectations of the narrator's mother to emphasize the fact that she is 'short and chubby' and her appearance is not what was expected.
'...or the glamorous teenage sister I had in mind'	
'She was dressed in drab gray pyjamas'	

6 How writers influence their readers

Learning focus:

- Considering the ways in which a writer can influence a reader
- Exploring how a writer engages a reader

The ability of a writer to engage a reader is crucial. The writer will want to influence a reader and make them react to what they have written. A piece of writing may be tense and generate suspense in the reader or it may work to elicit different emotions altogether. Humour, sadness, **empathy** and drama are all possible reader outcomes when reading a text.

Key terms

Empathy: the ability to share or understand another person's feelings.

Activity 1

a. Read the extract below carefully and think about how the writer influences the reader.

Memoirs of a Geisha by Arthur Golden

In this extract the narrator (Chiyo) and her sister have been taken from their homes and sold to different households in Kyoto, a city in Japan. Chiyo is not received kindly by Hatsumomo, one of the older girls in her household.

"I can't see why you girls from fishing villages smell so bad. That ugly sister of yours was here looking for you the other day, and her stench was nearly as bad as yours."

I'd kept my eyes to the floor until then; but when I heard these words, I looked Hatsumomo right in the face to see whether or not she was telling me the truth.

"You look so surprised!" she said to me. "Didn't I mention that she came here? She wanted me to give you a message about where she's living. Probably she wants you to go find her, so the two of you can run away together."

"Hatsumomo-san –"

"You want me to tell you where she is? Well you're going to have to earn the information. When I think how, I'll tell you. Now get out."

I didn't dare disobey her, but just before leaving the room I stopped, thinking perhaps I could persuade her.

"Hatsumomo-san, I know you don't like me," I said. "If you would be kind enough to tell me what I want to know, I'll promise never to bother you again."

Hatsumomo looked very pleased when she heard this and came walking toward me with a look of luminous happiness on her face. Honestly, I've never seen a more astonishing looking woman. Men in the street sometimes stopped and took their cigarettes from their mouths to stare at her. I thought she was going to come whisper in my ear; but after she'd stood over me smiling for a moment, she drew back her hand and slapped me.

"I told you to get out of my room, didn't I?" she said.

I was too stunned to know how to react. But I must have stumbled out of the room, because the next thing I knew, I was slumped on the wood floor of the hallway, holding my hand to my face.

Activity 1 continued

b. Now make a list of any feelings you experienced as you read this extract.

Activity 2

Answer the following questions, using evidence from the text to support your answer.

1. What do you think when reading what Hatsumomo says to Chiyo at the beginning of this extract?

----

2. Why do you think Chiyo had 'kept' her 'eyes to the floor' until that point?

----

3. Why does her response change to looking Hatsumomo 'right in the face'? What does this make you think about her?

Activity 2 continued

4. How is Hatsumomo trying to make Chiyo feel in the paragraph starting "You look so surprised!"?

   ----

5. What do you think about Hatsumomo at this point?

   ----

6. Hatsumomo tells Chiyo she will need to "earn the information" she wants. How do you respond to this?

   ----

7. What were your thoughts and feelings about Hatsumomo when she slapped Chiyo?

   ----

8. How would you compare Hatsumomo's behaviour to her appearance?

   ----

9. Throughout the passage how does the writer influence the reader's feelings towards Chiyo? Use evidence from the text to support your answer.

Unit 3: Assessment Objective 4

7 Bringing the writer's craft together

Learning focus:

- Exploring the ways a writer uses language and structure to achieve effects and influence readers
- Revising techniques already learned and thinking about how to combine them

Activity 1

Read the following summary of how writers use language and structure to achieve effects and influence readers, then fill in the blanks. You can use earlier work in the chapter to help you.

1. When looking at language I will study how a writer has used ———— and phrases to create —————.

2. The ————— of a piece of writing refers to the way in which the writing has been ordered. A writer deliberately ————— their writing to influence meaning and its effect.

3. The effect created by a writer refers to the way words and ————— are used deliberately to create an —————.

4. A writer uses their writing tools (language, structure, devices etc.) to ————— a reader. I will need to show how they use those tools to affect the way a reader may ————— to the text.

Activity 2

Read the extract carefully and think about the exam-style question below.

> How does the writer make this part of the story tense and dramatic? **[10]**

Activity 2 continued

Birdsong by Sebastian Faulks

In the following extract Jack Firebrace is part of a team of men who are digging a tunnel in order to blow up German soldiers and equipment during the First World War. The Germans are tunnelling towards them to attempt to do the same damage to British forces. One of the team has heard irregular noises against the wall of the tunnel.

Jack placed his head against the wall of the tunnel. He could hear the rhythmic gasp of the bellows in the overhead hosepipe draped from the ceiling. "You'll have to turn off the air supply, sir," he said to Weir.

"Christ," said Turner, "I can't breathe."

Weir dispatched a messenger to the surface. Two minutes later the noise ceased and Jack knelt down again. His exceptional hearing was frequently in demand. [...]

The men stood motionless as Weir held his finger to his lips. Jack breathed in deeply and listened, his body rigid with effort. There were sounds, distant and irregular. He could not be sure what they were. If they evacuated their tunnel as a precaution and the noise turned out only to have been shellfire or surface movement then time would be lost on their own tunnel. On the other hand, if he failed to identify German digging coming back the other way, the loss of life would be greater. He had to be sure.

"For God's sake, Firebrace." He heard Weir's hissing voice in his ear. "The men can hardly breathe."

Jack held up his hand. He was listening for the distinctive knocking made by timber when it was hammered into place against the wall. If a tunnel was very close it was also sometimes possible to hear the sound of spades or of bags of earth being dragged back.

There was a thumping noise again, but it did not sound hollow enough for wood; it was more like the rocking of the earth under shellfire. Jack tightened his nerves once more. His concentration was interrupted by a noise that sounded like the delivery of a sack of potatoes. Turner had collapsed on to the tunnel floor. Jack had made up his mind.

He said, "Shellfire."

"Are you sure?" said Weir.

"Yes, sir. As sure as I can be."

"All right. Tell them to turn the air supply on again. Firebrace, you get back [...]. You two, get Turner on his feet."

Activity 3

a. Now read the following student answers that have been marked and the commentary from the examiner.

> Evidence choice is appropriate, but the explanation is quite vague.

> Evidence choice is appropriate but the identification of these as emotive words seems strange. There is little attempt to explore the stillness implied by 'motionless'.

The writer makes this part of the story dramatic as to what happens because of the use of emotive words such as 'The men stood motionless' which makes you imagine the men standing there. Also the story is dramatic when 'there were sounds, distant and irregular', which makes you wonder what the sounds are.

The story is dramatic when it says 'there was a thumping noise again' as to what or who it can be making the noises. In addition the story is dramatic as it says 'Jack tightened his nerves once more' which makes it dramatic as you can feel it must be very scary.

Lastly the ending lines of the story are very dramatic and tense as 'Jack had to make up his mind' to what the banging was. When he replied 'shellfire' everyone could calm down to go back to work, which was a relief for there to be no Germans trying to get underground and also a relief to not have been found.

> This is a valid evidence selection and it does create drama, but there is more to say here. Why does this add drama? How is imagery used to demonstrate Jack's tension here?

> This is valid evidence, but there is so much more that could be said in relation to this.

Examiner comment

The candidate demonstrates some sense of the question here – there is regular focus on the drama of the situation. There is an attempt to engage with the issue of 'how' through the use of evidence and some commentary, but the explanation does not develop to really demonstrate an understanding of how language is used. 5 out of 10 marks.

Activity 3 continued

The candidate provides immediate focus on the question and then goes straight to the evidence.

The candidate focuses on the language and the writer's technique in order to make a clear point.

The candidate shows a clear awareness of structure.

Tension and drama are created as Jack immediately makes the others wait by placing his 'head against the wall of the tunnel'. The writer then describes him hearing the 'rhythmic gasp of the bellows' of air and lengthens the time before he speaks, creating tension. Jack's words suggest danger by telling the man in charge that he'll 'have to turn off the air supply'. This sense of danger is increased by Turner stating that he 'can't breathe'. Time is obviously important and the writer details how long it takes for Jack to be back listening, 'two minutes later the noise ceased'. The limited action between the messenger being 'dispatched' and Jack kneeling 'down again' emphasise that these actions take place quickly. We know that Jack's 'exceptional hearing was frequently in demand', which increases the tension because we wonder how many times he had needed to listen for strange noises and what they would do if they didn't have him to do this. Tension is raised as Weir tries to keep the men silent by holding 'his finger to his lips'. This suggests that he is trying to keep both himself and his men quiet to the point of not breathing. Jack even seems to hold his breath – he 'breathed in deeply and listened' to avoid making any additional noise. The pressure on Jack is suggested because if they evacuate the tunnel they might lose time 'on their own tunnel', which could help the Germans. If he doesn't evacuate though and the noise is German diggers 'the loss of life would be greater'. Tension is increased as we realize the importance of his decision. The writer affirms this with a deliberate short sentence: 'He had to be sure.' Weir hurries him up and the fact that he is described as 'hissing... in his ear' uses onomatopoeia to make a loud sound in what was a silent tunnel – this emphasizes the urgency of Weir's words. 'The men can hardly breathe.' Jack tries to listen again, tightening 'his nerves', which suggests that he is finding the pressure of the situation difficult. When Turner collapses, this hurries him to a decision. He confirms it is 'Shellfire' with a very definite one-word sentence. There is no room for doubt once a decision is made and the one word emphasizes his certainty. The tension dissolves as it is 'business as usual' and everyone goes back to where they were.

The regular use of the word 'suggests' shows the candidate is trying to comment on the impact of the writer's language.

The candidate is clearly aware of the effect this piece has on the reader.

The candidate makes clear points, supported by evidence, then drills into the evidence to explain how the writer uses language to make something dramatic.

Examiner comment

This candidate is clearly engaged with the question throughout. A range of points are covered as they track through the text. Insight into technique and the use of language is clear. Specific detail is combined with an overview of the passage and the question as a whole. 10 out of 10 marks.

b. Now you have read both answers, annotate the first one in three places to show how you would improve it.

Activity 4

Now it is your turn to answer this type of question.

a. Read the extract below carefully.

>
> *Enduring Love* by Ian McEwan
>
> What we saw when we stood from our picnic was this: a huge grey balloon, the size of a house, the shape of a tear drop, had come down in the field. The pilot must have been half way out of the passenger basket as it touched the ground. His leg had become entangled in a rope that was attached to an anchor. Now, as the wind gusted, and pushed and lifted the balloon towards the escarpment, he was being half dragged, half carried across the field. In the basket was a child, a boy of about ten. In a sudden lull, the man was on his feet, clutching at the basket, or at the boy. Then there was another gust, and the pilot was on his back bumping over the rough ground, trying to dig his feet in for purchase, or lunging for the anchor behind him in order to secure it in the earth. Even if he had been able, he would not have dared disentangle himself from the anchor rope. He needed his weight to keep the balloon on the ground, and the wind could have snatched the rope from his hands.
>
> As I ran I heard him shouting at the boy, urging him to leap clear of the basket. But the boy was tossed from one side to another as the balloon lurched across the field. He regained his balance and got a leg over the edge of the basket. The balloon rose and fell, thumping into a hummock, and the boy dropped backwards out of sight. Then he was up again, arms stretched out towards the man and shouting something in return – words or inarticulate fear, I couldn't tell.

10 minutes

b. Now answer the question below using all that you have learned about analyzing how writers use language and structure to achieve effects and influence readers.

> How does the writer make this scene tense and dramatic? **[10]**

Start your answer here and continue on blank paper if necessary.

Activity 4 continued

Support

Reread your answer carefully. Check you have considered the following:

1. Is your answer logical and organized? Have you tracked through the text sensibly?

2. Have you used evidence to support your ideas?

3. Have you explained why the selected evidence makes the scene tense and dramatic?

4. The writer's use of language – why are specific words/phrases important?

5. How does the writer create effects?

6. Does the structure of the piece add to the tension/drama?

7. Does the writer try to influence the reader?

Use this checklist and spend another 10 minutes trying to improve your answer.

8 Personal and critical evaluation

Learning focus:

- Exploring ways to **evaluate** texts critically
- Revising techniques for personal response
- Focusing on supporting ideas with textual references

Key term

Evaluate: to form an idea of the state or value of something.

If an exam question seeks a personal response from you then you will need to show that you can assess what you have been reading and come to a sensible judgement about it. To really show your skills you need to show how the writer led you to that judgement.

Tip

In an exam if you need to demonstrate that you can critically evaluate a text you need to:

- look at specific detail
- examine evidence
- show how you have come to a judgement by linking these together.

Activity 1

a. Read the extract below carefully.

Galloping Foxley by Roald Dahl

The narrator recalls some of his worst memories from attending boarding school. Foxley was a prefect at the school and the narrator is one of the junior boys who had to carry out his orders. Foxley was authorized to beat the junior boys if they did not do whatever he told them to do. He had a particular grudge against the narrator and made his life miserable.

But the worst memories of all had to do with the changing room.

I could see myself now, a small pale shrimp of a boy standing just inside the door of this huge room in my pyjamas and bedroom slippers and brown camel-hair dressing gown. A single bright electric bulb was hanging on a flex from the ceiling, and all around the walls the black and yellow football shirts with their sweaty smell filling the room, and the voice, the clipped, pip-spitting voice was saying, 'So which is it to be this time? Six with the dressing-gown on – or four with it off?'

I never could bring myself to answer this question. I would simply stand there staring down at the dirty floor planks, dizzy with fear and unable to think of anything except that this other larger boy would soon start smashing away at me with his long, thin, white stick, slowly, scientifically, skilfully, legally, and with apparent relish, and I would bleed. Five hours earlier, I had failed to get the fire to light in his study. I had spent my pocket money on a box of special firelighters and I had held a newspaper across the chimney opening to make a draught and I had knelt down in front of it and blown my guts out into the bottom of the grate; but the coals would not burn. [...] I wanted desperately to answer because I knew which one I had to choose. It's the first thing you learn when you arrive. Always keep the dressing gown on and take the extra strokes. Otherwise you're almost certain to get cut. Even three with it on is better than one with it off.

'Take it off then and get into the far corner and touch your toes. I'm going to give you four.'

Activity 1 continued

b. In an exam you might be asked a number of questions to test your own personal response to a text or how you would evaluate it. For example, in response to this extract you could be asked:

1. How do you react to Foxley and to what takes place in these lines? **[10]**

2. How does the writer encourage the reader to feel sympathy towards the narrator? **[10]**

3. What are your thoughts and feelings about the way the narrator is treated? **[10]**

Choose one of questions 1–3 and complete the following table.

Chosen question:	
Evidence	**Evaluation – how do you react and what judgement does that lead you to?**
E.g. 'a small pale shrimp of a boy standing just inside the door of this huge room'	E.g. I feel sorry for the narrator. His appearance makes him sound young and weak. His small size is emphasized by his comparison to a 'shrimp' and the immediate contrast that follows between his diminutive size and that of the 'huge room'. We immediately get the impression of someone who is out of his depth.

Activity 2

a. Below is one student's response to the first question. Read it carefully and then look at the examiner's comment that follows.

> How do you react to what takes place in these lines? **[10]**

Student answer

In these lines a 'small pale shrimp of a boy' is standing inside a 'huge room'. He is wearing 'pyjamas and bedroom slippers' and 'a brown camel-hair dressing gown'. Someone is speaking to him with a 'clipped voice'. He asks whether he wants 'six with the dressing gown on' or 'four with it off'. The boy could not 'bring' himself to 'answer the question'. He just stood staring at the 'dirty floor planks'. He can't think about anything other than the 'larger boy... smashing away' at him. He remembers that he had 'failed to get the fire to light in his study'. He wants to answer and choose the 'extra strokes' because 'even three' with the dressing gown on 'is better than one with it off'.

Examiner comment

This candidate does not really answer the question. The candidate seems to be answering a question about what takes place in the text, rather than giving a reaction to what takes place. There is some knowledge of the text and the candidate isolates some useful evidence, but the explanation needs to respond to what the question is asking for.

b. Annotate the answer to show how this candidate could alter their work to answer the question.

Activity 3

On the next page is the beginning of a strong answer to the second question. Look at what the student has done so far and see if you can complete this answer.

> How does the writer encourage the reader to feel sympathy towards the narrator? **[10]**

Activity 3 continued

Student answer

We are immediately ready to hear a story that generates sympathy for the narrator because he starts by referring to what is to follow as being one of 'the worst memories of all'. He remembers himself as a 'small pale shrimp of a boy', which highlights his diminutive size and encourages the reader to feel sorry for him.

That he is 'pale' suggests that he is perhaps feeling unwell, generating sympathy, and the comparison to a shrimp further emphasizes his smallness. The immediate contrast between this small boy and the 'huge room' that he is 'just inside the door' of also emphasizes his relative size and we feel sympathy because he seems to be intimidated.

Activity 4

a. Read the following extract carefully.

The 2½ Pillars of Wisdom by Alexander McCall Smith

Three professors from the Institute of Romance Philology attend their annual conference, choosing to stay in a family-orientated hotel.

Prinzel had arrived first, and taken the best room, the one with the uninterrupted view of the lake. He had felt slightly uneasy about this, as it was a room which should really have gone to von Igelfeld, who always got the best of everything [...]. For this reason Prinzel was careful not to mention the view and contrived to keep von Igelfeld out of his room so he could not see it for himself. Unterholzer, who always got the worst of what was on offer, had a slightly gloomy room at the side of the hotel, above the dining room, and his view was that of the hotel tennis court.

'I look out onto the tennis court,' he announced one evening as the three gathered for a glass of mineral water on the hotel terrace. [...]

Then Prinzel had an idea. Tennis did not look too difficult; the long summer evening stretched out before them, and the court [...] was empty.

'We could, perhaps, have a game of tennis ourselves,' he suggested.

The others looked at him.

'I've never played,' said von Igelfeld.

'Nor I,' said Unterholzer. 'Chess, yes. Tennis, no.'

'But that's no reason not to play,' von Igelfeld added quickly. 'Tennis, like any activity, can be mastered if one knows the principles behind it. [...] What could be simpler?'

Unterholzer and Prinzel agreed, and Prinzel was despatched to speak to the manager of the hotel to find out whether tennis equipment, and a book of the rules of tennis, could be borrowed. The manager was somewhat surprised at the request, but in an old hotel most things can be found and he eventually came up with an ancient dog-eared handbook from the games cupboard. This was *The Rules of Lawn Tennis* by Captain Geoffrey Pembleton [...] published in 1923, *before the tie-breaker was invented*.

[...]The three professors strode confidently on to the court. Captain Pembleton had thoughtfully included several chapters describing tennis technique, and here all the major strokes were illustrated with little dotted diagrams showing the movement of the arms and the disposition of the body.

It took no more than ten minutes for von Igelfeld and Prinzel to feel sufficiently confident to begin a game. Unterholzer sat on a chair at the end of the net, and declared himself the umpire. The first service, naturally, was taken by von Igelfeld, who raised his racquet in the air as recommended by Captain Pembleton, and hit the ball in the direction of Prinzel.

The tennis service is not a simple matter, and unfortunately von Igelfeld did not manage to get any of his serves over the net. Everything was a double fault.

'Love 15; Love 30; Love 40; Game to Professor Dr Prinzel!' called out Unterholzer. 'Professor Dr Prinzel to serve!'

Activity 4 continued

Prinzel, who had been waiting patiently to return von Igelfeld's serve, his feet positioned in exactly the way advised by Captain Pembleton, now quickly consulted the book to refresh his memory. Then, throwing the tennis ball high into the air, he brought his racquet down with convincing force and drove the ball into the net. Undeterred, he tried again and again after that, but the score remained obstinately onesided.

'Love 15; Love 30; Love 40; Game to Professor Dr von Igelfeld!' Unterholzer intoned. 'Professor Dr von Igelfeld to serve!'

And so it continued, as the number of games mounted up. Neither player ever succeeded in winning a game other than by the default of the server. At several points the ball managed to get across the net, and on one or two occasions it was even returned; but this was never enough to result in the server's winning a game. Unterholzer continued to call out the score and attracted an occasional sharp glance from von Igelfeld, who eventually suggested that *The Rules of Tennis* be consulted to see who should win in such circumstances.

Unfortunately there appeared to be no answer. Captain Pembleton merely said that after six games had been won by one player this was a victory – provided that such a player was at least two games ahead of his opponent. If he was not in such a position, then the match must continue until such a lead was established. *The problem with this, though, was that von Igelfeld and Prinzel, never winning a service, could never be more than one game ahead of each other.*

This awkward, seemingly irresoluble difficulty seemed to all of them to be a gross flaw in the theoretical structure of the game.

'This is quite ridiculous,' snorted von Igelfeld. 'A game must have a winner – everybody knows that – and yet this... this *stupid* book makes no provision for *moderate* players like ourselves!'

'I agree,' said Prinzel, tossing down his racquet. 'Unterholzer, what about you?'

'I'm not interested in playing such a flawed game,' said Unterholzer. [...]

They trooped off the tennis court, not noticing the faces draw back rapidly from the windows. Rarely had the Hotel Carl-Gustav provided such entertainment for its guests.

b. Now answer the exam question that follows, using the lines on the next page.

> How do you react to what takes place in these lines?
>
> You should write about:
>
> * what takes place in these lines
> * the characters
> * the writer's use of humour [10]

Activity 4 continued

After you have undertaken the preparation suggested in the tips box, give yourself 10 minutes to answer the question.

Tips

It may help you to proceed as follows:

- Reread the question. Underline any key words that may help you to focus on what is expected of you, e.g. How do you react...

- As you read the extract, underline or highlight evidence that you will use to answer this question.

- Reread the question again. Begin your answer by focusing carefully on what the question has asked, e.g. My reaction to what takes place in these lines...

Progress check

You have revised how to evaluate a text critically and give a personal response. Tick the box which you think best indicates your progress:

I am working to improve my knowledge of this skill.	
I have achieved this in places and will practise this skill further through wider reading.	
I am confident that I have achieved this skill and will implement it in wider reading.	

Component 1 Section B: Writing

Summary of Component 1 Section B: Writing

Component 1: Whole paper
• 40% of total marks for GCSE English Language
• Assessment length: 1 hour 45 minutes
• Section A – Reading
• Section B – Writing

Section B
• Half marks for Paper (20% of total grade)
• Complete ONE writing response from a choice of four titles
• Time required: 45 minutes including time to plan and check work

Section B of Component 1 tests your ability to craft a narrative account of approximately 450–600 words in length. You need to write in a sustained way to produce writing that is engaging and coherent.

Section B is worth half of the marks available for Component 1 and is marked out of a total of 40 marks. 24 of the marks are awarded for how well you communicate and organize your ideas. The other 16 marks are available for effective vocabulary choices, controlling and varying sentence structure, accurate spelling and punctuation.

Assessment Objectives

Section B of the Component 1 exam (Writing) tests your abilities in the following assessment objectives (AOs):

AO5	Communicate clearly, effectively and imaginatively, selecting and adapting tone, style and register for different forms, purposes and audiences.
	Organize information and ideas, using structural and grammatical features to support coherence and cohesion of texts.
AO6	Use a range of vocabulary and sentence structure for clarity, purpose and effect, with accurate spelling and punctuation.

1 Planning to write

Learning focus:

• Understanding the exam requirements of Component 1 Section B Writing

There are a number of things to keep in mind when you complete your writing for the Component 1 exam. This section will help you revise them and focus your skills to help you get the best grade possible.

✏ Activity 1

Look at the list of things below about the writing part of Component 1. Tick all of the things you know are true. Use page 41 to help you find the answers.

1. I am given a choice of four titles. ☐

2. I should write about all of the titles given. ☐

3. I will have about 45 minutes in total to complete my writing. ☐

4. I should choose one of the titles. ☐

5. Planning is not essential as I'm marked on how much I write. ☐

6. 16 of the 40 marks available are for vocabulary, sentence structure, spelling and punctuation. ☐

7. Planning will help to show I'm in control of the direction of my writing. ☐

8. Anything I write about must be true. ☐

9. I should avoid overly personal narratives, text language and inappropriate content as these won't score highly. ☐

10. I must show the examiner every single writing skill I can think of. ☐

11. My writing needs to be between 450–600 words. ☐

12. I should describe settings, develop characters and show clearly how events fit together in a plot. ☐

Tip

Having a clear dilemma or problem in your story helps to give it focus as the reader wants to know how it will be solved.

Key term

Motivation: what a character wants to get/do/achieve. Your reader needs to understand what your character wants to achieve if they are going to sympathize with them or see their point of view.

Activity 2

a. Look at the writing ideas below. Choose one. Let your interest and personal experience lead you. Remember you can use personal experience or write imaginatively.

> EITHER Write about a time when you were scared.
>
> OR Write a story ending with the words 'I never saw it in quite the same way again.'
>
> OR Write a story starting with the words 'I'd been warned not to…'
>
> OR Write a story with the title 'The birthday present'. **[40]**

b. Fill in the planning table below to help you generate ideas for your writing.

Writing idea chosen:			
Character 1	**Character 2**	**Key settings:**	**Plot:**
Name:	Name:	1.	Problem or dilemma:
Appearance:	Appearance:		
Personality:	Personality:	2.	Resolution:
Motivation:	Motivation:		

Activity 2 continued

c. Swap your table with a partner. Read through their notes and check they make sense. Are there any problems or areas that could be improved? Write some short feedback.

_____

_____

_____

_____

_____

d. When you have received feedback from your partner, complete the work review below.

List two positive things about your plan.

Point 1:

_____

_____

_____

Point 2:

_____

_____

_____

Identify one thing you need to keep in mind to help you in the final exam:

_____

_____

_____

2 Openings

Learning focus:

- Revising different ways of opening a narrative
- Writing an effective opening paragraph

Activity 1

The opening of your writing is very important. Unscramble the anagrams below to give reasons why.

a. Openings can <u>ohok</u> _ _ _ _ _ the reader straight into the action.

b. Openings can establish the <u>domo</u> _ _ _ _ _ and style of your writing.

c. Openings should <u>moepris</u> _ _ _ _ _ _ _ _ good things to come.

d. Openings can set up a <u>bomprel</u> _ _ _ _ _ _ _ _ to be solved.

e. Openings might introduce a key <u>recatchra</u> _ _ _ _ _ _ _ _ _ _ or setting.

Activity 2

Below is a list of six different ways of opening a narrative.

1. A strong statement
2. A problem
3. An interesting scene
4. A question
5. Dismissing a common view
6. An anecdote or brief story.

The openings below and on the next page are responses to the question:

> Write a story ending with the words, '...I couldn't believe they could be that cheeky.'

Match each of these openings to the six methods above. Write the number in the box next to them.

a. Why did they do it? I suppose I'll never know. ☐

b. At the time it happened I was in year 7 and I had no idea about how girls could be so vicious. ☐

Activity 2 continued

c. The teacher's eyes were so wide I thought they would shoot out across the room. We all sat there in disbelief. Mr bright spark fell from the top of the class like a dying star. ☐

d. Girls can be devious. Boys just knock each other out if they've got a grievance, and then it's all over. Girls – well, the plotting for revenge can go on for months... ☐

e. Simon hurried along the corridor. He knew he was going to be late. Yet he had little knowledge at that point of the consequences those extra five minutes styling his hair would have. ☐

f. We're all under the impression that friends shape our lives for the better. But that's rubbish! Friends can be warm, loving creatures – the source of all life's joy, but they can just as easily suck you dry of all your patience, time and energy. ☐

Activity 3

Look again at the openings in Activity 2. Explain which one you like best. You might make this decision based on which one does all of the things listed in Activity 1 or you might judge it based on which one makes you want to read on.

My favourite is _____

I liked this opening most because _____

_____

Activity 4

Now you are going to try to write your own openings for this title:

Write about a time when you were successful.

Activity 4 continued

a. Begin by making some notes to answer these questions to give direction to your writing.

i. What was the success?

----

ii. Why is it worth writing about? What made it special?

----

iii. What other key details will be essential in the story?

----

b. Below are each of the six different opening types and space for you to trial your own.

i. a strong statement

----

ii. a problem

----

iii. an interesting scene

----

iv. a question

Activity 4 continued

v. dismissing a common view

----

vi. an anecdote or brief story

----

c. Now either share your openings with a partner or review them yourself to choose which one is best. Again, use the list in Activity 1 or your own judgement to decide.

d. Use this opening and complete the story.

Progress check

Tick the correct box for each skill to record your progress

Skill being tested	I am working to achieve this skill	I have achieved this skill in places	I'm confident I've achieved this skill
Writing an opening to hook the reader			
Writing an opening to establish the mood			
Writing an opening to promise good things to come			
Writing an opening that sets up a problem to be solved			
Writing an opening which introduces a key character or setting			

3 Organizing and structuring

Learning focus:

- Revising ways of organizing and structuring work
- Writing narrative using different organizational methods and a light tone

Activity 1

There are lots of decisions you can make about how you organize your writing. Sometimes these are personal preference but they definitely need to fit the story you are writing. Match up the organizational features below to the explanations of what they can do. The first one is done for you.

1. Chronological

2. Flashback

3. Foreshadowing

4. Trigger

5. **First-person** narrator

6. **Third-person** narrator

7. A frame

a. A clear question or statement at the beginning of your writing, and an answer or reflection at the end. This can give a neat opening and closing and shows clear thinking about the direction of the writing.

b. The person telling the story is a character involved in the events. 'I was ...'.

c. The narrative goes back to a previous time – recent events or further back in a person's life.

d. Something which prompts a flashback. For example, in the film *Batman Begins*, seeing the bats in the opera takes Bruce Wayne's mind back to vivid memories of the bats in the well.

e. The narrative is told either by a person not involved in the events or an outside 'godlike' voice who sees and knows everything: 'She was ...'.

f. The events follow on in a normal time sequence.

g. A clue is given to something that will happen later in the narrative.

> **Key term**
>
> **First-person (I/we):** using first-person narrative allows you to tell a story from the perspective of a character in the text.
>
> **Third-person (he/she/it/they):** using third-person narrative means the story is told from an independent point of view so you can see what all the characters think and feel.

Activity 2

Look at this exam-style question:

Write about a day that you didn't want to end.

Use the space below to map out your ideas in a spider diagram. Consider the four ideas given, as well as your own:

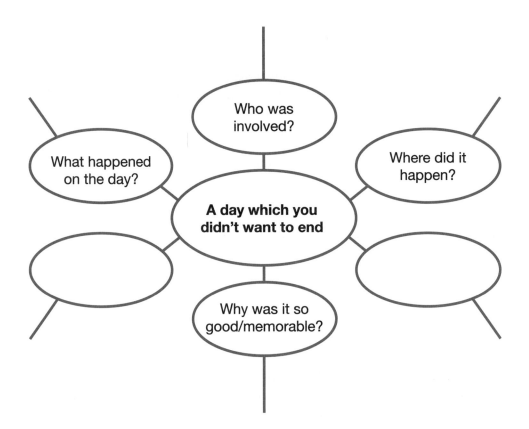

Activity 3

In the extracts below, a student has written about a day they did not want to end. These extracts are taken from the beginning, middle and end of their work. They have used some of the seven techniques listed in Activity 1 for organizing their work. Annotate the sample with the techniques you find and comment on what you think they add to the writing.

Why is it when you're young that Christmas is just so magical? Is it the belief in Santa or that parents just go out of their way to make sure everything is just perfect for you? I remember one Christmas when I was 7 that was so memorable I think it epitomizes the snow globe Christmas scene. My own bike-crazed perfect Christmas scene anyway.

... The delights just kept on coming. My mum – sneaky Christmas elf lady – suggested that I opened the curtains in the living room while she got out some bowls for breakfast. I didn't protest but was a little bemused: normally she tells me to stay away from them for fear of me pulling the not-so-smoothly-running bay-window pole out of the plaster like my dad's nearly done in rage a few times. What met my eyes as I opened the window made all the mystery unravel though. Perched up against the garden fence was a shiny new blue road bike. At the time I guessed it was just too big for Santa to steer down the chimney.

... So nine years on I know I won't really experience any Christmas Days full of that same childlike wonder and magic, but they're still fun times spent with family. This year mum's promised that we'll all go out ice-skating in the city centre on Boxing Day. Secretly, I think she fancies herself as Elsa. Maybe I'll buy her an adult version of the costume to bring out a bit of that particular Disney magic in her!

Activity 4

The tone of the student sample extract on page 51 is quite witty. This endears the first-person narrator to you and helps you imagine the day as they see it.

a. Find examples of the following techniques that create this light tone.

i. Giving extra personal detail to clarify an idea

----

ii. Parenthesis to give extra character detail (here in paired dashes)

----

iii. Humorous details about an action that give a sense of different character

----

iv. Using hyphens to make a phrase with lots of detail

----

v. Going into the mind of the character at the time

----

vi. Sharing a 'secret' with the reader

----

b. Look back at the plan you made in Activity 2. Which of the techniques above can you use to keep the tone light while picking up marks for varying your sentence structure and vocabulary? Choose two of the techniques and draft your own ideas.

Technique:

My draft:

Activity 4 continued

Technique:

_____

My draft:

_____

_____

_____

_____

_____

Activity 5

Bearing in mind what you have practised, spend 35–40 minutes completing your writing about a day that you did not want to end. Consider which of the different organizational techniques from Activity 1 on page 49 will work in your writing.

1. Chronological

2. Flashback

3. Foreshadowing

4. Trigger

5. First-person narrator

6. Third-person narrator

7. A frame

Look back at the tips on varying vocabulary and sentence structure in Activity 4 to keep your tone light and witty.

Make sure you leave yourself 5 minutes to check your work at the end.

You can use the lines on the next page for your writing.

Stretch

If you are using complex sentence structures, it can be easy to lose the thread of your point, or jumble what you are saying. Make sure you check:

• that punctuation is accurate

• that ideas are clear and can be followed through the sentence

• the sharpness of your expression (could you be more focused with stronger vocabulary choices, for example?).

✏ Activity 5 continued

Progress check

Tick the correct box for each skill to record your progress

Skill being tested	I am working to achieve this skill	I have achieved this skill in places	I'm confident I've achieved this skill
Using different techniques (like flashback, a trigger, foreshadowing) to structure writing			
Considering the effects different techniques will have on my reader to decide which is best to use			
Using a light/witty tone to draw the reader to the narrator			

4 Developing the narrative: settings

Learning focus:

- Revising how to develop a narrative
- Focusing on details of settings
- Planning and writing a narrative that focuses on detail in settings

Activity 1

Settings are very important in a narrative, as they not only help your reader to imagine a place but they also give a sense of the mood. As a reminder of some of the techniques to help you develop settings, complete the sentences below.

a. S_____s and m_____s can help your reader through the comparisons they draw but should be used sparingly.

b. Making your reader use some of their five s_____s through the description makes them imagine the setting vividly.

c. Precise and varied v_____y helps to give detail.

d. V_____s and ad_____s are especially good at adding a sense of movement but can also describe how something sounds or feels.

Activity 2

The description of a setting below was part of a student's response to a task with the title, 'The sale'.

> Their are people everywhere, it is very busy. People shout from the market stalls, their voices are loud. The smell of burgers from the grill floats across the air. I can see my mum between the brown coats of old ladys with headscarves.

Activity 2 continued

The student sample on the previous page is an example of writing in band 2. The examiner's comments below are taken from the mark scheme.

a. Find an example from the student's writing that you think matches each comment. Annotate the work with the numbers below.

1. Some control, coherence and organization.

2. Communication is limited but clear.

3. Some variety of sentence structure.

4. Spelling is usually accurate.

Support

There are two spelling errors and two punctuation errors in the student's response. Can you find them?

Stretch

This student makes the same punctuation error twice by using a comma in the first two sentences. This is a common error students make. Which piece of punctuation should replace the comma to show the ideas are linked?

b. Now look at the annotated work below.

The student could introduce a list here with a colon or add a simile to get a sense of how packed the place is.

What do they shout? Using direct speech here to give a voice to the different market traders' calls could really bring the piece to life.

Semi-colons are needed here to link the ideas, not commas.

Their are people everywhere, it is very busy. People shout from the market stalls, their voices are loud. The smell of burgers from the grill floats across the air. I can see my mum between the brown coats of old ladys with headscarves.

Simple comment but still relevant to the question.

Two simple spelling errors here: the homophone 'there' is misspelt as the possessive 'their' and the plural rule for y has not been followed to give 'ladies'.

How does this smell make the narrator feel? Hungry? In need of some fresh air?

How does mum interact with the old ladies? Do they jostle her for a place in the queue? Are they calm and orderly?

Activity 2 continued

c. Use the prompts and ideas in the annotations on page 56 to rewrite this setting in a much more interesting way.

----

d. Thinking about the work you have just done, give yourself marks for AO5 and AO6. Take your reasons from the marking criteria.

AO5 mark = _____

Reasons: _____

_____

AO6 mark = _____

Reasons: _____

_____

One reason the Activity 2 response was in band 2 was its lack of purposeful control. Lots of different ideas were lumped together in one paragraph. The band 4 criteria on organization says the narrative will be 'purposely shaped and developed'. One way to show purposeful shaping is to think of each little part of a setting being described as a photograph. Then when you move from that part you can use a **preposition** to guide your reader to the next one. For example:

- In front was the ...

- Beside the stall was a ...

- On the roof ...

- Underneath all of this ...

Tip

Don't overuse prepositions at the start of sentences. You need to show a variety in your sentence structures.

Key term

Preposition: words, like 'in', 'on', or 'over' that connect a noun, noun phrase or pronoun to another word.

Activity 3

a. Choose one of the exam-style questions below.

> Write about a time when you had to make a difficult decision. **[40]**

> Write a story starting with the words, 'It started as a normal day but...' **[40]**

b. What settings would you need in your story? Write them below.

----

c. Now choose one of your settings. Make sure you know what you want your reader to feel about this place before you write. Guide your reader using prepositions as you describe three parts of the setting.

Activity 4

Plan the rest of the narrative that you chose in Activity 3 using the space below. You could use a table like that on page 43 or a spider diagram. Focus on making your settings really vivid. You can use the setting you wrote in Activity 3 or improve it.

When you have finished your plan, write your full answer on separate paper. Spend no longer than 45 minutes planning, writing and checking your work to give yourself a real sense of how long you have got in the exam. Remember to take extra care checking your punctuation to ensure your writing is controlled and makes sense.

5 Developing the narrative: characters

Learning focus:

- Revising the rules for punctuating speech
- Developing characters through speech and **implicit** detail

Activity 1

a. The **vowels** have been removed from the rules for punctuating speech below. Add them in.

   i. K__p th_ w_rds th_t are sp_k_n _ns_d_ th_ _nv_rt_d c_mm_s.

   ii. K__p th_ p_nct__t__n f_r th_ sp__ch _ns_d_ th_ _nv_rt_d c_mm_s.

   iii. St_rt _ n_w p_r_gr_ph f_r __ch n_w sp__k_r _r th__r _ct__ns.

b. The passage of speech below has had all speech punctuation and paragraphing removed. Use the rules above to write it correctly.

> Positively skipping, he screeched What a delight, what a delight! My dear you just will not believe the honour. I watched him. Lords he added. I said nothing. Lords! Home of afternoon tea and the most English game he added. I sighed basket weaving? His face dropped. No, my dearest cricket.

Support

Try to imagine the conversation to help you decipher who says what. There are seven paragraphs altogether. Look carefully at the last three sentences to make sure you assign the right speaker to the correct words.

Stretch

The narrator's silence in this exchange is quite powerful. What does it add to the narrative?

As illustrated by the passage in Activity 1, speech can give information about events to other characters, and to the reader. It also helps to develop a reader's understanding of a character. By not saying anything in response to the man, the narrator appears strong and perhaps also a little impatient. No one has used those words but the implicit detail comes across in the way the speech is written.

Activity 2

a. Decide on a time when you felt angry. This will be the topic of your writing for this section of work. The rest of the prompts below will help you think carefully about your **dialogue**.

----

i. Where will there be dialogue in your story? Maybe there is an argument or an intense conversation which provokes your anger?

----

ii. What will you want to show about the characters involved in the dialogue? Are you both angry? Does the other character realise they have made you angry?

----

b. Now write a short stretch of dialogue from the planning notes above. Remember to vary your **speech tags**: 'said' can get very repetitive. Make sure you include important implicit details to suggest things about your character's personality or motivation.

Tip

Remember that silence can be powerful. It might be more interesting to show your anger through actions rather than cursing or immature language like 'I hate you.'

Key terms

Dialogue: the words spoken by people in a piece of writing.

Speech tags: these indicate dialogue and tell you how the words are spoken, i.e. 'said', 'shouted' or 'whispered'.

Activity 3

The way settings are described can also tell you about the character's priorities and views. In the passage below, Mia, a young girl, admires the beauty of a valley in the Lake District. Mia is not the narrator but we see the setting through her eyes.

a. Read the extract below carefully.

It was like nothing she'd ever experienced before. Sure – Mia had seen hills in her life: her house perched on the top of the tallest rise in her village, as she was reminded each time she had to push her bike home. But these majestic giants, rising from the mists, were something other-worldly to her.

Here, in this valley, the peaks rose up in sharp ascent. Cloud rested on their heads like unruly hairdos. These giants sat, as if at a dinner or in conference, around a dark mystical lake. Mia noticed the occasional bubble or ring rise to the surface, and anticipated (almost dared to wish) that magical creatures would erupt from the surface at any minute.

b. Now answer the questions that follow.

i. Pick out five things Mia admires in the place she has visited.

---

ii. What are the clues in the way the passage is written that tell you that she likes these things?

---

iii. What does liking these things suggest about Mia's character?

Activity 3 continued

c. To practise using setting to convey details about a character, write a third-person description of yourself looking around a sibling's or a friend's room. Look from the outside at yourself, just as the narrator watches Mia. Select details that will give clues about the personality of who is looking at the room as well as who owns it. Think about what you might compare it with in order to give the viewpoint of the observer – like Mia compares the majestic, other-wordly peaks of the valley with her small hill at home.

Activity 4

45 minutes

Now gather up what you have learned so far about using speech and setting (pages 55-63) to develop a sense of character.

> Write a story starting with the words, 'They never meant it really...'

Plan your response carefully:

- What was it that 'they' did or said but didn't mean? Will you say what it is in the opening paragraph or hint at it to keep your reader guessing?
- What characters will you need to describe and what sort of detail will you want to suggest about them?
- Where will you include dialogue? How can the dialogue you write also give details about the characters?
- What settings will your narrative need? How can you make these work to give details about the characters who are in them or who describe them?
- How will your narrative end?

Use the space below for your planning and write your answer on separate paper.
Spend 45 minutes, including planning, writing and checking to help you get a feel for the timings for the exam.

6 Effective endings

Learning focus:

- Considering how to write an ending to suit the content and style of the story
- Practising writing an end that clearly tells the reader the writing is finished

When you write an ending to a piece of writing there are two main jobs it needs to do:

1. Signal clearly to the reader that the writing is finished with a reflection on what has happened or a neat summary.

2. Tie up ends by answering questions posed in the writing OR reflect on the opening OR leave a cliffhanger and a sense that what is written is part of a bigger story.

Activity 1

The endings below complete a narrative called 'The time traveller'. Assess them against the two criteria above.

In the lines underneath, reflect on which ending you think is best and why.

Ending example	Does it clearly signal the end?		What type of ending?		
	Yes	No	Ties up ends (Resolution)	Reflects on opening (Circular)	Cliffhanger
A: And that's how he went on. His job was never finished; his energy never faltered. Maybe he'll enter your town one day. Who knows…					
B: I noticed every small detail of his appearance when I finally met the time-travelling stranger. He walked up to me and asked, 'Can I come and meet your friends?'					
C: So that was it really. As I said at the start – not all stories can have a happy ending. But mine did.					
D: As much as we'd believed in his story, we'd been taken in by his lies. He wasn't our saviour and he was certainly not our friend. He'd left us desolate and destroyed.					

Reflection:

✏ Activity 2

You've already looked at some types of endings in Activity 1. It is important that you consider the impact the type of ending has on your reader. Match up the endings below with the types of reactions they might provoke.

Types of ending	Possible reactions
Circular	A sense of complete satisfaction because questions have been answered or problems solved
Resolution	A sense of excitement or wonder as the story seems to continue into the unknown
Cliffhanger	A sense of agreement with the writer's earlier thoughts or understanding of their **perspective**

✏ Activity 3

45 minutes

Now use what you have learned in this chapter to complete one of the following narratives.

> **EITHER**, Write a story ending with the words, '... I turned away and didn't look back.'
>
> **OR**, Write a story with the title 'The mysterious figure.'
>
> **OR**, Write about a time when you were helpful.　　　　[40]

Spend 10 minutes planning your work. Carefully consider what type of ending it will have and how you will lead up to it. Write up your work in 35 minutes on separate paper. Make sure you leave yourself time to check the accuracy of your writing.

Tip

When you have an ending line given to you in the exam-style question, you do need to use it! Part of the skill is how you craft your story so that the words you have been given feel like a natural conclusion to your writing, not ones stuck on as you have been told they must be there.

Progress check

a. Swap your narrative with a partner. Read through the story and give it a mark for AO5 and AO6. Note at least two things they did well and two areas that could be improved.

b. When you have received your feedback, go through their notes. Choose one area you would like to focus on to improve.

   Rewrite a paragraph, taking their advice on board.

c. Review your new paragraph. Do you think you have improved? Consult your partner again for their feedback if you are unsure.

Key term

Perspective: a particular way of thinking about something

Component 2 Section A: Reading

Summary of Component 2 Section A: Reading

Component 2: Whole paper
• 60% of total marks for GCSE English Language • Assessment Length: 2 hours • Section A – Reading • Section B – Writing
Section A
• Half marks for Paper (30% of total grade) • Short and long answers • Time required: 1 hour (approximately 10 minutes reading and 50 minutes answering questions)

Section A of Component 2 will test you on your ability to read and understand two non-fiction texts. One text will be taken from the 19th century and the other will be taken from the 21st century. The texts will be linked by a topic or theme. You will be assessed on your understanding of the two texts, your ability to combine information from the texts and your ability to compare them.

Section A is worth half of the marks available for Component 2 and will be marked out of a total of 40 marks. You will be expected to answer a series of structured questions based on the two passages.

Assessment Objectives

Section A (Reading) of the Component 1 exam will test your abilities in the following assessment objectives (AOs):

AO1	Identify and interpret explicit and implicit information and ideas. Select and synthesize evidence from different texts
AO2	Explain, comment on and analyse how writers use language and structure to achieve effects and influence readers, using relevant subject terminology to support their views.
AO3	Compare writers' ideas and perspectives, as well as how these are conveyed, across two or more texts.
AO4	Evaluate texts critically and support this with appropriate textual references.

Unit 1: Assessment Objective 1

1 Location of explicit details

Learning focus:

- Revising reading techniques
- Revising how to identify explicit information and ideas
- Considering how to present the information located

This section will guide you through the skills you will need to approach a Reading text in Component 2. You will complete a number of activities that will help you to revise how to locate explicit information and ideas within a text before practising answering this type of question yourself.

Activity 1

Before you start to locate information in a text, you need to know exactly what you are looking for. Read the example questions below carefully and highlight the keywords (they will help you understand what to look for and how to present your answer).

1. List **five** reasons why the workers decided to go on strike.

2. What reasons are given in support of safe swimming?

3. Where can you find guidance about free running?

Example:

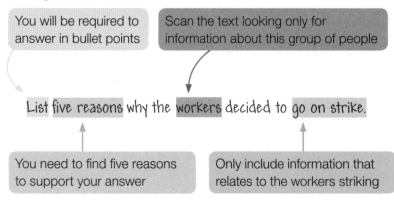

You will be required to answer in bullet points

Scan the text looking only for information about this group of people

List five reasons why the workers decided to go on strike.

You need to find five reasons to support your answer

Only include information that relates to the workers striking

Activity 2

a. Read the following extract from *The Times*.

> **'CCTV Britain, the world's most paranoid nation'**
> The stall was the kind you often see in the countryside in summer, selling surplus produce from someone's garden: a glut of green beans, a few misshapen courgettes. There was the usual "honesty box" into which to push your coins. But beside it was a notice: "You are being watched" and an arrow pointing upwards to a security camera's all-seeing eye. Cycling back through the sweet-smelling Suffolk lanes, I felt rather bleak. The stall was beside a Norman church in the sleepiest village. The sum at risk was just a few quid. The camera didn't appear to be plugged in. But that didn't matter. The point was even in this lovely, remote and – to my city mind – innocent place, CCTV had once again replaced trust. [...]
>
> Whether we are buying a sandwich, taking a bus or visiting the doctor we have become relaxed about our presence being recorded.

The questions below will require you to locate specific details from the extract. Read each question and then **scan** the text looking for keywords to help you work out where to locate the correct details. You might like to use a highlighter to indicate the key details from the text.

b. Where is the writer cycling?

_____

c. List three places where, according to the writer, you can be filmed by CCTV.

_____

_____

_____

d. What reason does the writer give for feeling "rather bleak"

_____

_____

Key term

Scan:
look quickly through a text to find specific details, rather than reading it closely to take in all the information.

Activity 3

In the exam you have to work out how to present the information and how much to include. Using the questions for Activity 2 to help you, write down two pieces of advice to help you when answering this type of question. For example, if you are asked to list information you should use bullet points in your answer.

1. _____

   _____

2. _____

   _____

Activity 4

Sometimes you may be asked to locate a number of details from across a whole text.

a. Read the extract below carefully.

> *The Complete Notes* by Bill Bryson
>
> I was heading for Newcastle, by way of York, when I did another impetuous thing. I got off at Durham, intending to poke around the cathedral for an hour or so and fell in love with it instantly in a serious way. Why, it's wonderful – a perfect little city – and I kept thinking: 'Why did no-one tell me about this?' I knew, of course, that it had a fine Norman cathedral but I had no idea that it was so *splendid*… So let me say it now: if you have never been to Durham, go at once. Take my car. It's wonderful.
>
> The cathedral, a mountain of reddish-brown stone standing high above a lazy green loop of the River Wear, is, of course, its glory. Everything about it was perfect – not just its setting and execution but also, no less notably, the way it is run today. For a start there was no nagging for money, no 'voluntary' admission fee. Outside, there was simply a discreet sign announcing that it cost £700,000 a year to maintain the cathedral and that it was now engaged in a £400,000 renovation project on the east wing and that they would very much appreciate any spare money that visitors might give them. Inside, there were two modest collecting boxes and nothing else – no clutter, no nagging notices, no irksome bulletin boards or stupid Eisenhower flags, nothing at all to detract from the unutterable soaring majesty of the interior. It was a perfect day to see it. Sun slanted lavishly through the stained-glass windows, highlighting the stout pillars with their sumptuously grooved patterns and spattering the floors with motes of colour. There were even wooden pews.

I'm no judge of these things, but the window at the choir end looked to me at least the equal of the more famous one at York, and this one at least you could see in all its splendour since it wasn't tucked away in a transept. And the stained-glass window at the other end was even finer. Well, I can't talk about this without babbling because it was just so wonderful. As I stood there, one of only a dozen or so visitors, a verger passed and issued a cheery hello. I was charmed by this show of friendliness and captivated to find myself amid such perfection, and I unhesitatingly gave Durham my vote for best cathedral on planet Earth.

When I had drunk my fill, I showered the collection pot with coins and wandered off for the most fleeting of looks at the old quarter of town, which was no less ancient and beguiling, and returned to the station feeling simultaneously impressed and desolate at just how much there was to see in this little country and what folly it had been to suppose that I might see anything more than a fraction of it in seven flying weeks.

Bill Bryson is clearly impressed with the city of Durham, especially the cathedral. Use the table below to write down reasons why he is so impressed.

Sometimes candidates focus on only one area of a text. By separating your ideas in the table below, you will be able to record a range of things that impress Bryson.

Feature of Durham	Why is Bryson impressed?
Durham (itself)	'a perfect little city'
Cathedral	
People	

Activity 5

Now try to write up an answer to the following question. Your challenge is to complete your answer in less than ten minutes and to include a wide range of details from the text, so try to be economical with your words.

> What reasons does Bill Bryson give to show that he is impressed with Durham? **[10]**

Bill Bryson is immediately impressed, calling Durham 'a perfect little city' and...

----

2 Location and interpretation of implicit details

Learning focus:

- Revising how to identify and **interpret implicit** information and ideas
- Exploring ways to discuss and present the information

In an exam you may need to explore some of the explicit information you find to show that you understand the wider implications and meaning in a passage. Usually questions relating to interpreting information require you to make **inferences** about the information you have read. Making inferences requires close reading of the text and then an interpretation of any relevant details.

Activity 1

Question stems for interpretation questions may include the words listed below.

Write a definition of each keyword or phrase.

a. Explain…

----

b. Why…

----

c. What impressions…

Activity 2

a. Read the extract below carefully.

'Adam Richman's Fast Food Filth'

Man v Food is [...] a food reality series that follows Adam Richman, a guy with a self-professed "serious appetite" around the United States as he gorges on some of the most calorific and ridiculously portioned food in the world.

[...] some of the challenges Adam Richman has attempted to complete include: eating a 2kg steak; a 7.5lb hamburger; 17 hotdogs; 2 gallons of ice cream; a 10-course meal and 10 grilled cheese sandwiches with toppings. [...]

I do not enjoy, at all, watching the overweight and certainly unhealthy Adam Richman stuff his face with thousands of calories and celebrate like it's some sort of triumph. [...] It makes me feel a bit sick to witness this celebration of such an unhealthy and indulgent approach to food. [...] Since when did food become a conflict to be overcome, where the only prize is obesity?

There's something seriously wrong with firstly: allowing someone to promote their love for a vile and unhealthy lifestyle on television and secondly: society's acceptance of this because he's a funny bloke. This show seems to be demonstrating everything that's wrong with our attitudes towards food. [...] Not once on the show have I heard anything about the importance of an active and healthy lifestyle, 5-a-day may as well apply to the amount of meals he recommends and there no disclaimer to say to the audience: don't try this at home. [...]

Thinking about the kinds of people that watch this show, if they're young and impressionable, [...] chances are they'd love to go and see how much they can eat in half an hour before spending the evening crashed out on the sofa feeling sluggish. Restaurants, before long, will start creating their own food "challenges" and that would be disastrous. [...] People in Third World countries don't even have enough food for one day, and yet somehow it's acceptable for First World inhabitants to waste food and gorge themselves into a life of high blood pressure, obesity and heart attacks. Something is wrong. [...]

Entertaining or not, Man v Food is disgusting and dangerous as is its star Adam Richman. America, you can keep your backwards, unhealthy and indulgent TV shows; Jamie Oliver is just one example of someone who has spent years trying to make a difference in the way we eat as a country and Adam Richman is on his way to undermine all of that. Don't expect obesity levels to decrease in any country if you're giving shows such as this one airtime. We're living in a contradiction and it's time that changed.

Activity 2 continued

b. Now read the exam-style question below. The keywords have been highlighted for you. Make a note about what each of these requires you to focus on.

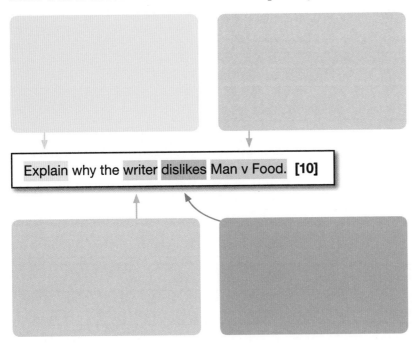

Explain why the writer dislikes Man v Food. **[10]**

c. Complete the following table.

Quotes showing the writer's dislike for Man v Food	If relevant, give a reason to explain why this shows the writer dislikes it.

Activity 2 continued

d. Now use the information from the table to help you write up your answer. Think about which of these reasons may require more explanation than some of the others. Try to be economical with the quotations and number of words you use in an explanation.

----

e. Review your answer by ticking the following boxes.

1. Did you approach the text chronologically? ☐

2. Did you cover details from each paragraph/area of the text? ☐

3. Are your quotations brief but still make sense? ☐

4. Have you written an explanation next to any quotations that require inference? ☐

5. Does your answer link back to the question you have been set? ☐

Activity 3

a. Read carefully the letter below, written in the 19th century, about ragged schools, which details some of the general problems faced by poor children.

[...] There are hundreds of poor children who have either no home to go to, or such an one as you would fear to enter; that many pass the night under arches, or on the steps of doors, or wherever they can – poor unhappy little beings! Oh! When you pray for yourselves, and ask God to bless your father and mother, your brothers and sisters, then do not forget to ask Him also to help the poor outcasts.

Now, Ragged Schools have been set on foot by kind and Christian people on purpose to do good to these unhappy children. They are brought to these schools, and there they have their torn, dirty clothes taken off, and after being washed, and made nice and clean, they have others put on to wear all day, but at night they are obliged to have their dirty ones put on again, because their parents are so wicked, that if they went home in good clothes they would take them from them and sell them, and spend the money on something to drink. Then they would send the children out again in miserable and filthy rags, or nearly without clothes at all; so the kind people at the schools take care of the clean clothing for them at night. The children stay at school all day and have food provided for them. Sometimes they have one thing, sometimes another. The day I was at Dr Guthrie's school, they had each a basin of nice hot soup and a good-sized piece of bread. What a treat for these poor, neglected, hungry things! Perhaps you, my young friends, never knew what it was to want a morsel of bread. It is a terrible thing to be very hungry and to have nothing to eat; a terrible thing to see the shop windows full of nice bread, and cakes, &; to be very, very hungry, and to have no means of obtaining anything but by stealing [...]

b. Now read the exam-style question below.

Look at the text from 'Now, Ragged Schools' onwards. What impressions do you get of the lives of children who attend ragged schools? **[10]**

c. Write an answer to the exam-style question above. Remember to include details from the text to support your answer and refer to the question.

_____

_____

_____

_____

_____

Activity 3 continued

Activity 4

a. Read the following student answer to the exam-style question.

It is unquestionable that the 'poor unhappy little beings' have a rotten life. Many are homeless or have a home as 'one as you would fear to enter'. We learn that the children are 'unhappy', suggesting their lives are pretty miserable. The children are not well clothed as their clothing is described as 'torn, dirty clothes'. Their lives sound cruel as their selfish parents are described as 'wicked' people who take away their children's clean clothing (as provided by the ragged school) and would sell them to gain money for 'something to drink'. The children sound neglected, 'nearly without clothes at all' and sound as though they have parents who care very little for them to 'send the children out again in miserable filthy rags'. The children are described as 'poor, neglected, hungry', making their lives sound pitiful.

Activity 4 continued

b. Can you match each of the comments below to the relevant section of the answer? Add them to the annotation boxes provided.

1. The student does well here to include a couple of references to the text as well as some inference (all within one sentence).

2. The student does well again by including two clear references to the text and supporting inferences (all within one sentence).

3. This has been taken from the first paragraph and students were instructed to begin their answer from 'Now, Ragged Schools'. No credit would be given for this section of the answer.

4. The student concludes with another clear inference and a supporting quotation.

5. This is a simple inference and is well supported by relevant evidence.

Stretch

Can you think of any additional ideas from the text that the student could have included in this answer?

----

3 Combining information from two texts

Learning focus:

- Revising how to select key details from two texts and then **synthesize** this evidence into one document

When asked to synthesize information from two texts, you must read each text carefully and then select and combine specific information in an answer. Read the question through carefully to help you narrow down the information you require. Highlighting key details as you read will help you to be selective in your answer.

Key term

Synthesize: to combine or put together.

Activity 1

a. Read the two texts about playgrounds carefully. Both writers suggest the playgrounds are areas where children are happy and have fun. The first text was written in the 19th century. The second is a modern text.

> ### 'Walks in and around London'
>
> A little while ago this bright spot was a sad, dull and melancholy waste… But wise and kind-hearted people have levelled and laid it out as a garden and playground for the little ones. Here, strolling along its sanded walks, which go winding a round beds of bright-looking and sweet-smelling flowers; or stopping to watch the jet of water flung into the air from the fountain and dropping back into the basin where the gold and silver fish dart to and fro; or leaning back in the comfortable seats like real ladies and gentlemen, the myriads of children from the courts and alleys around, as well as those just let out from school, come to forget the hardness of their life in the beauty and merriment of the playground.
>
> Some of you whose friends bring you so many grand toys, would not look at the things that bring these poor children such enjoyment. An old shuttlecock with one solitary feather in it, picked up from some dust-heap, is batted into the air with a piece of cardboard. A paper Windmill bought for a farthing, which mother has squeezed out of her hard earnings, delights that little three-year-old boy as he holds tightly in his chubby fist. His clothes are ragged and torn, yet I'm sure his mother is kind to him. He has found out that by holding the mill straight in front of him, the wind catches the bright-coloured sails and spins them round till the colours run into one another and he sees only a rainbow-coloured ring in front of him. So, forgetting the big boots shaking about on his feet, he trots up and down, laughing so merrily.

Activity 1 continued

> **'Withy Grove Play Area'**
>
> Withy Grove Play Area at Bamber Bridge, situated in Lancashire, is certainly one of the UK's best free parks. The park itself is huge and divided into sections for different age groups. From large sandpit play areas for younger children to skate ramps, zip lines, tube slides and an epic climbing area, there really is something for everyone.
>
> What was once a desolate field, is now a source of entertainment and huge fun. Not only is there ample parking in the nearby leisure centre car park, but it is close to the M6 and easy to access. In the summer months the park is crammed with happy families, some of whom even bring a bucket, spade and packed lunch. For those looking for a horticultural experience then this park is not for you. Although the park has been tastefully landscaped, the focus here is on fun, fun fun!
>
> Don't believe me? Why don't you come and see for yourself? The smiles you will see on every face you pass are testimony to this park's success.

b. Now read the exam-style question below.

> According to these two writers how do you know that children enjoy visiting parks? **[4]**

c. Use the following table to jot down three key details from each text.

How do you know that children enjoy visiting parks?	
Evidence from 'Walks in and around London'	Evidence from 'Withy Grove Play Area'

Tip

Note the mark tariff. This question is worth 4 marks so you only need to select a few details from each text.

Activity 1 continued

d. Now that you have selected some key details, think about how you can link the information together to write a full answer to the question. You might start with something like:

Both texts show children get a great deal of pleasure from parks. In the first text...

Use this beginning to complete your own answer in the space below.

Activity 2

Now look at the mark scheme below for this question. A range of details are required in order for you to achieve more than one mark. You need to make sure you include sufficient details so that you are able to show the examiner that you have understood both the question asked and the texts you have read.

Mark	Criteria
0	Nothing worthy of credit
1	Some selection of relevant details from both texts
2	Selects a range of relevant details from both texts
3	Synthesizes with some understanding a range of relevant detail from both texts
4	Synthesizes with clear understanding a range of relevant detail from both texts and provides an overview drawn from relevant detail from both texts

Thinking about the full answer that you produced in Activity 1, try to see where your answer would fit against the criteria.

Activity 3

Producing an **overview** is quite challenging. An overview is a summary of something and it must be both brief and succinct. Read the following overviews that were produced in response to the question in Activity 1.

1. Which one best provides an overview of the two texts? Try to match the overview with the correct comment below.

Overview	Comment
The two parks are not only available to all but they provide a safe, aesthetically pleasing environment for children and their families to play in.	This overview is neat and succinct but it focuses on parks in general, not whether children enjoy going there
The two parks bring a great deal of fun to the families who visit, with the first text suggesting the 'laughter' and 'merriment' that can be heard at the park and the second suggesting 'fun', 'entertainment', and as it is 'crammed' it must be extremely popular too.	This is a very focused sentence in which the candidate brings the two texts together but also manages to support the answer with numerous references to the texts
The two parks sound like they are fun places. The two parks seem like they have been purpose-built to encourage a great deal of fun and enjoyment. Parks should all have this as their vision but some do not seem to take into account the many different users that a park will have. While it is positive that the first park provides 'merriment' this is tinged with sadness as the 'merriment' is only a temporary escape from their sad lives.	The candidate has lost focus on the question here and is writing at length about issues that are not relevant

Unit 2: Assessment Objective 2

4 How writers use language

Learning focus:

- Revising how to comment on, explain and analyse how writers use language, using relevant subject terminology
- Making sure language/text analysis remains purposeful and relevant to the task set

✏ Activity 1

Read the extract below carefully.

> **'Just how good is the modern TV?'**
>
> By 1970 almost 90 per cent of all homes had a television, but with only three channels and a relatively small screen, it is difficult for many modern TV fanatics to imagine just how far the humble television has come in the last 40 years.
>
> With high-resolution, panoramic, curved screen 3D televisions that not only show hundreds of channels but can be used to watch shows 'on demand', to surf the internet, to play games and even monitor your health, modern televisions are an essential way of life, not just something we can watch for half an hour. We are addicted to them because they literally offer so much.
>
> Last week, Dr Johnson (although he could be a doctor of seal studies in the Sudan), slammed the modern TV for making us lazy and obese. Does he have a point? He claims we are so seduced by what the modern TV can offer that we have become a slave to its functions. Johnson claims that anyone who watches more than an hour a day is an 'addict' and ought to cut back on their viewing immediately. But those of us who are firmly fixed to our TVs would prefer him to keep his views to himself. The modern TV is amazing, wonderful and quite literally as the TV Times claims, an entertainment package for the whole family. A few hours a night is not an addiction, it's absolute bliss, it's escapism and it's brilliant...
>
> Ted Knowles

Tip

When you are asked to consider 'how' a writer achieves an effect or influences the reader, you will need to consider the language, structure, tone and effects used by the writer. Some candidates will simply spot devices and write down relevant subject terminology but the best candidates will consider the effect of these devices and will link their ideas back to the question.

A number of different questions could be asked about this brief text. One mistake made by students when they read the word 'how' is that they don't read the rest of the question and then produce a generic answer with no real focus. Work through the following activities carefully to help you write meaningful answers that link to the question.

Activity 2

You could be asked the following question:

How does the writer persuade us that the modern TV is 'essential'? **[10]**

This text contains a wealth of language and techniques that persuade us that modern TV is amazing. Complete the following grid by adding four examples of your own.

Example of language	How does this persuade you that modern TV is 'essential'?
'addicted to them' ~~[crossed out]~~	This sounds like our lives depend on them and that we can't live without the TV
'high resolution, panoramic curved screen 3D TV's'	". Adjectives make TV sound appealing
'essential way of life"	Sounds like that one can't live without TV
"it's absolute bliss, it's ~~[crossed out]~~ it's brilliant" escapism	Adjectives and wide range of vocab make it sound that TV is essential
* Today, I am *	

Activity 3

The writer is clearly impressed by the modern TV. How does the writer persuade us that the modern TV is impressive?

Look at the table overleaf and complete it to show that you can select the correct evidence and make a meaningful comment on the techniques the writer has used.

Activity 3 continued

Example of language	Technique/method	Link/effect
'only three channels and a relatively small screen… just how far the humble television has come'	Compares past to present	The comparison shows modern TV is impressive as so many huge developments have been made.
'high-resolution, panoramic, curved screen 3D televisions	Lists a wealth of positives ~~and vices~~	The adjectives show how impressive TV is
'Dr Johnson (although he could be a doctor of seal studies in the Sudan)~~...~~ Does he have a point?	Uses an anecdote to undermine what the doctor claims	Undermining the Doctor Proves that TV is essential
	Rhetorical question	The reader questions whether the doctor's claims are valid in an attempt to make their own argument seem more balanced.
'TV Times claims, an entertainment package for the whole family.'	Expert opinion	Using evidence to convince the reader
'A few hours a night is not an addiction'	Repeats key phrase	Emphasising the point that TV is important
'it's absolute bliss, it's escapism and it's brilliant…'		

Tip

The text has been explored chronologically. Tracking the text makes it easier when structuring a clear answer.

Activity 4

a. Using the information in the table in Activity 3 and your own ideas, write up a response to the question:

> The writer is clearly impressed by the modern TV. How does the writer persuade us that the modern TV is impressive? **[10]**

1.) By the writer comparing the past with the present he shows that TV is impressive as so many huge developments have been made.

2.) When the writer lists a wealth of positives the adjectives show how impressive TV really is

Activity 4 continued

b. To make sure you have remained focused on the technique we used in Activity 3, go through your answer and highlight the following in three different colours:

- the evidence you have used
- the techniques you have mentioned
- the areas where you explain the effect or link your ideas back to the task.

Activity 5

Having revised some of the techniques we can use when analysing a text (for example language, lists, repetition, etc.), make a list of any other areas you can comment on in a 'how' question. A couple have been added for you.

- Tone
- Structure
- *Emotive*
  emotive Language
- *Personification*
- *Subversion*
- *Satire and Parody*
  & Political

Activity 6

a. Read the extract below carefully.

> **'Not all reality TV is ruining today's youth'**
>
> We have all become accustomed to the continual criticism of reality TV and how it is dangerous to young people. Critics have claimed that the stars of these shows set the example of irresponsible behaviour, and have a regrettable impact on impressionable young people. Those who support TV however, suggest that this is not the case with all shows – quite the opposite. Several shows are renowned for promoting the right qualities. Take *Junior Apprentice* for example. It can be said that it helps children learn about the world of business and encourages the development of a range of positive qualities such as: attention to detail, confidence in leadership, and the skills required to speak in front of their peers. These skills are essential life skills that will prepare them in many ways for the world of work. TV role models can teach a child many things, such as empathy, social skills and the value of being considerate in society.

Activity 6 continued

There are also programmes that families can all watch together, such as *Mythbusters* or *How It's Made*. These spark the imagination by introducing new places, ideas, by de-mystifying science or glorifying travel and adventure. They also introduce kids to real issues in an informative way. Reality TV is a different way of exposing kids to big topics because it focuses on real people going to real places and doing real things. It can be extremely motivational. Interesting and engaging human stories can also be explored through reality TV. This can be seen in shows like *Real Lives* for example, where two teams of inspirational people race around the world facing local customs, navigation challenges, clues and mental struggles.

The problem lies in encouraging young viewers to choose shows like the more sensible *Cake Boss* instead of the controversial *Real Housewives*. It's difficult. Young viewers have been conditioned to get hooked into idiotic drama, drunken mishaps and awkwardly embarrassing personal situations and it's a challenge to persuade them to break the mould and see that there are other options for their viewing. For the networks, money is all, and this comes from high viewing figures – quality often doesn't come into it when they know that over-the-top drama will bring in more viewers.

Unfortunately, this means that most networks will continue to focus on a successful formula of providing cringe-worthy and senseless reality shows rather than ones that educate, inform and inspire.

b. Now read the exam-style question below.

> How does the author persuade us that 'not all reality TV is ruining today's youth? **[10]**

c. Use the information/techniques you know about answering a 'how' question to answer the exam-style question above in exam conditions.

When the writer says "attention to detail, confidence in leadership and the skills required to speak in front of their peers" he lists a great deal of positives which help emphasise that not all reality TV is ruining today's youth.

Activity 6 continued

Progress check

Mark	Features of answer	My mark
0	Nothing written Not relevant to the question	
1	One or two simple comments/minimal evidence Copying Little focus on the question	
2–4	Simple comments / few details Aware of obvious meaning or persuasive methods Can be unselective (long quotes/chunks of text) Some spotting of techniques (not explained)	
5–7	Valid comments based on valid textual details Some spotting of factual details Some awareness of writer's method/ language with some reliance on spotting key words/phrases	
8–10	Explore the text in detail Valid comments/inferences Able to combine specific detail with some overview Understanding of persuasive methods/language	

a. Look at your answer from Task c. in Activity 6 and the marking grid above. Allocate yourself a mark by ticking one of the boxes.

b. Write down three things that you need to remember the next time you complete a 'how' question.

Point 1 _____

_____

Point 2 _____

_____

Point 3 _____

_____

Unit 3: Assessment Objective 3

5 Comparing information and ideas from two texts

Learning focus:

- Revising how to compare ideas across two texts
- Revising how to present these comparisons

Comparison questions are usually at the end of a reading examination, as by this point you will have read both texts and should be familiar with their contents. There are usually two parts to making comparisons: firstly, comparing ideas and secondly, comparing how the ideas are presented. This section will focus on both of these skills.

✏ Activity 1

a. Read the two texts about clothing choices carefully.

> **'What to wear? ' by Ruth Margolis**
>
> My daughter has already developed a penchant for princesses, but she also loves dinosaurs, fire trucks, and trains. Can I find the latter on girls' clothing in any major chain store? Nope. Instead, I'm presented with racks of pastels and glitter. If there's an image on a shirt, it's probably a female Disney character with a dainty chin, invisible waist, and giant eyes. Should I want any kind of vehicle, or an animal that isn't a cutesy bird or cat, it's over to the boys' aisle, where everything is so overpoweringly masculine I can feel hairs sprouting on my cheeks.
>
> Where are the pale pink t-shirts with monster trucks? What I wouldn't give for an embroidered diplodocus on a skirt… It's also hard to find plain clothing that would work for a boy or a girl.
>
> […]
>
> If retailers would only lead the way in reassuring us that it's acceptable to dress our kids how we actually want to. Of course, many parents would stick rigidly to the outmoded and heavily gendered 'rules', but others would branch out and, in doing so, part with a bunch of money. Perhaps they'd also teach their kids that clothing doesn't have to describe their sex.
>
> […]
>
> I'm not interested in telling parents how to dress their children. And I wouldn't dream of stomping on my own child's own dream to own a fairy princess outfit the colour of a popular indigestion remedy. But if she asks to twin it with shoes emblazoned with both trucks and hearts then I'd like to know where to shop for that.

Activity 1 continued

> *Men in Petticoats* edited by Peter Farrer
>
> Let them (men) take a leaf out of the reforming programme of women, who, when dissatisfied with any article of their own costume, bodily annex and wear in its stead such garments of the opposite sex as we desire. As for myself, I wear the male hat, tie, colour, cuffs, coat, and a vest, as well as the 'unmentionables', though the latter are not quite in evidence as yet. These portions of men's costume I, together with a large number of women, have adopted because I am thoroughly disgusted with the dress of our sex, and hope for a still more sweeping reform than has yet been accomplished. I was brought up abroad, and have been through the whole process of figure training, having had while at school to wear stiff and heavily boned stays, as tightly laced as possible, both day and night, over which all the pupils had securely locked steel waist-belts, the keys of which were kept by the house governess, thus precluding the possibility of relaxation. And, although as a consequence, I have a very good figure and an exceptionally small waist, I long for the freedom of male attire.

b. Both writers give their views on the clothing available for females. Compare what the writers have to say about this topic.

Use the table below to note down what each writer has to say about the clothing available for females. The first one has been done for you.

'What to wear?'	Men in Petticoats
I'm presented with racks of pastels and glitter.	when dissatisfied with any article of their own costume…wear in its stead such garments of the opposite sex

c. Now look back through the details you have selected. Highlight any areas or ideas which are similar.

Activity 1 continued

d. Try to write down two or three words for each text that you feel gave the writer's overall opinion (this will help you to produce an overview when writing an answer).

Activity 2

a. Read the following student answers.

Student answer 1

The two writers do not like the choices of clothing that are presented to girls. It would seem that not much has changed over the last one hundred years because girls still want to wear boy's clothing as they do not like their own. In the first text, the writer does not like the colours selected for girls' clothing and she would like to see more neutral clothing available for both boys and girls. In the second text the writer shares her thoughts on how uncomfortable female clothing was and how many women long to wear men's clothing. The first text shows how the writer would support clothes that could be used for boys and girls and the second shows how period clothing was both uncomfortable and restrictive for girls.

Student answer 2

The two writers do not approve of the girls' clothing that is presented to girls. The first writer does not like 'racks of pastels and glitter' as she questions 'Where are the pale pink t-shirts with monster trucks?' She also suggests that she would like more neutral clothing, 'plain clothing that would work for a boy or a girl'. The second writer also complains about women's clothing and suggests to 'wear in its stead such garment of the opposite sex' as she was 'disgusted with the dress of our sex'. Rather than complaining about colour though, she complains about clothing being oppressive and uncomfortable, 'stiff and heavily boned stays, as tightly laced as possible'.

The first text shows how the writer would support clothes that could be used for boys and girls and the second shows how period clothing was both uncomfortable and restrictive for girls. The first writer comments that she would like clothing to be more diverse, with 'shoes emblazoned with both trucks and hearts', showing a desire for compromise, while the second writer simply longs for 'the freedom of male attire'. Both writers are dissatisfied with the clothing available, with the first writer recognizing 'heavily gendered "rules"', and the second hoping for 'sweeping reform than has yet been accomplished'.

Activity 2 continued

b. Which answer do you think is most effective in answering the question? Give three reasons to explain your choice.

----

c. Go back through each answer and complete the following:

1. In one colour, highlight or underline any sections of the response where the student compares the texts or makes a cross reference.

2. In a second colour, highlight or underline evidence which has been taken from the text.

3. In a third colour, highlight or underline any overview points.

Stretch

It is not always easy to compare two texts in a short space of time. To develop this skill further, work with a partner and complete the following tasks:

a. Spend 2 minutes writing down a list of the key features of your school.

b. Go back to your list and write down what you think about each of the areas from your list.

c. First of all, compare the key features lists that you each compiled. Highlight which areas you have both selected and underline any that only one of you has included.

d. Now look at the opinions you have included about each feature. Go through the opinions and try to sort them into three areas:

1. Areas that you agree on

2. Areas that you disagree on

3. Areas that only one of you mentions

e. Spend 10 minutes collating all of your ideas into a piece of writing. Make sure you refer to evidence from the information you wrote down.

You can develop your ability to pick out similarities and differences by looking at different reviews of the same film, programme or book, comparing newspaper articles of the same topic and so on.

6 Comparing how the writers get across their views

Learning focus:

- Revising how to comment on and compare how two writers get across their views

To complete the second section of a comparison question, you need to compare how the writers get across their views. This section of the question requires you to look closely at the methods used by each writer and compare them.

Activity 1

Think about everything you have done in class about the writer's method and make a list of the possible techniques that you might look out for.

Activity 2

a. Read the two texts carefully.

'Walks in and around London'

A little while ago this bright spot was a sad, dull and melancholy waste… But wise and kind-hearted people have levelled and laid it out as a garden and playground for the little ones. Here, strolling along its sanded walks, which go winding a round beds of bright-looking and sweet-smelling flowers; or stopping to watch the jet of water flung into the air from the fountain and dropping back into the basin where the gold and silver fish dart to and fro; or leaning back in the comfortable seats like real ladies and gentlemen, the myriads of children from the courts and alleys around, as well as those just let out from school, come to forget the hardness of their life in the beauty and merriment of the playground.

Activity 2 continued

'Vandalised playground swings back into action'

Children can finally get to grips with new equipment at a play area three months after vandals set fire to the facility. A total of £53,000 was spent at the playground to repair the vandalized items and improve the equipment and grounds. The play area now boasts a basket swing and traditional swing set, a large net, an aerial runway, a rope bridge and a new slide. It was officially opened on Thursday.

Councillor Bob Timbs said, 'It was disappointing Dene Road was hit by vandalism, but I am pleased we were able to repair the equipment rather than replace it. I am delighted this play area is now open and being used by young children in the area.' Vandals set light to the new climbing net at the Dene Road site on Thursday, March 24. It caused serious damage, which cost Oxford City Council £8,000 to repair. No one has been arrested in relation to the incident and officers were still keen to speak to a group of youths seen playing in the area shortly before the fire.

b. Complete the table below to collect evidence of the points of comparison between the texts.

Points of comparison	Evidence/comments from 'Walks in and around London'	Evidence/comments from 'Vandalised playground swings back into action'
Contents of the text		
Use of language		
Writer's opinion/view		
Purpose/aim of the text		
Tone of the text		
Structure of the text		
Audience for the text		

Activity 2 continued

c. Look again at the information you have included in your table. Are there any similarities and differences in the way in which the information is presented in the two texts? Use the table below to collect the points that are similar and the ones that differ.

Similarities	Differences

7 Comparing information and how writers get across their views

Learning focus:

- Revising how to compare ideas across two texts
- Revising how to comment on and compare how two writers get across their views

Now we will bring together both parts of the comparison question. In this unit you will compare the writers' ideas across two texts and will also consider how the writers get across their ideas.

Tip

Remember to include appropriate language when you are making a comparison: although, however, whereas, likewise, similarly, but, conversely, etc.

Activity 1

a. Read the two texts about chocolate carefully.

> **Chocolate: 10 health reasons you should eat more of it by Andrew Baker**
>
> Chocolate is the ultimate comfort food, a sure-fire stand-by in times of stress, a reliable source of consolation when life has let us down, and a mood-enhancer and romance-inducer in more positive circumstances. But is it at all healthy?
>
> If you scoff lots of it, obviously not. But there are a host of medically proven ways in which chocolate – good chocolate, which is to say dark chocolate, with a cocoa percentage of around seventy per cent or more – really is good for us.
>
> Research is continuing all the time, and experts have already found that chocolate is good for the heart, circulation and brain, and it has been suggested that it may be beneficial in such major heath challenges as autism, obesity, diabetes, Alzheimer's disease and even ageing in general.
>
> And in fact, the very latest research suggests that even milk chocolate may also provide valuable nutrients that lower the chance of heart problems.

Activity 1 continued

A GRAND COMBINATION.

The Typical English Game

of Football calls for greater muscular strength and activity than any other pastime, and it is important that those who indulge in it should prepare themselves by a proper diet. For this purpose there is nothing to equal Cocoa, which in its absolutely pure form, as in **CADBURY'S,** contains all the elements of strengh and vigour neccessary to give force and firmness to the muscles and nerves, and to impart staying power to the player. Before the game, it supplies a high degree of energy; after the game. it imparts a restful and comfortable feeling. Be sure, however, that you drink

"Cadbury's," the Typical English Cocoa.

b. Now read the exam-style question below.

> Both of these texts are about chocolate. Compare the following:
> * how the writers feel about chocolate
> * how the writers get across their views to the reader. **[10]**

c. Read through each text and write down two or three words that you feel summarize each writer's feelings about chocolate.

_____

_____

_____

d. Go through each text carefully and highlight any details that suggest what the writers think about chocolate.

e. Now think about each writer's method. Make a list of the ways in which they get their ideas across. Look at the list you made on page 95 to remind you.

_____   _____

_____   _____

_____   _____

_____   _____

_____   _____

> **Tip**
>
> Try to make sure your quotations are short but make sure that they also make sense.

Activity 2

a. Read the following student answer that has been marked and the commentary from the examiner.

Which details?

Andrew Baker immediately gives a positive view of chocolate as 'the ultimate comfort food' and gives specific details about chocolate that can be really 'good for us'. He clearly likes chocolate as he lists the parts of our body that benefit from eating chocolate. The Cadbury's text makes it sound like their cocoa is superior to all others and the writer clearly feels that it is an essential requirement for those engaging in exercise.

Where is your evidence?

How do you know?

Where is the evidence to support this?

Both Baker and the Cadbury's text get their message across by listing the many great benefits of chocolate. Both use positive language to describe chocolate and the tone of each text is both upbeat and positive. The purpose of Baker's text is to inform the reader, whereas the purpose of the Cadbury's text would have been to persuade people to buy the product and the use of pictures of footballers would also help this. Both texts appeal to the general public. Baker's text uses rhetorical questions that he then answers to ensure the reader is given plenty of facts about the benefits of chocolate. He also acknowledges the supposed disadvantages of eating too much chocolate and assumes that we all share his view. The Cadbury's text talks about a 'proper diet' and we are made to feel that cocoa would be a part of this. Baker uses a similar technique when he vaguely mentions that experts 'have already found that chocolate is good for the heart' but does not give any concrete evidence to support this. Both writers focus on the huge number of benefits that chocolate can bring to a person's health and this encourages us to share their positive view that it is good for us.

Example?

Such as?

How? You need to make this relevant to the second bullet.

How do you know?

How? Why?

Where? Example?

Where? Example?

But how does this get across their view?

Examiner comment

This is a promising answer but there are areas where the points made are not supported with evidence from the text. There are a number of clear comparisons and the answer is well-organized.

Activity 2 continued

b. Look at the answer on the previous page. The examiner has written a number of comments next to the answer. Read the comments and rewrite this answer by including the details the examiner has asked for. See if you can add any further comments to improve the answer.

----

c. When you have completed your answer, read back through it and highlight the following in different colours:
- any references to the writer or each text (this makes it clear for an examiner to follow your ideas from each text)
- any language you have used to compare the texts (whereas, like, etc.)
- any quotations you have included
- any references to the writer's method.

Activity 3

a. Read the two texts about poor living conditions carefully. The first is a modern text; the second was written in the 19th century.

'India's Slumdog census reveals poor conditions for one in six urban dwellers'

One in six urban Indians lives in slum housing that is cramped, poorly ventilated, unclean and 'unfit for human habitation', according to the country's first census of its vast slum population. In other words, nearly 64 million Indians live in a degrading urban environment very similar to the shantytowns portrayed in the Oscar-winning movie Slumdog Millionaire.

The first-ever nationwide report looks at urban slums in around 4,000 towns across India. (A slum was defined as a settlement of at least 60 households deemed unfit for human habitation, but the report does not cover every town and city in this vast country). [...] While the report described open sewers and poverty, it also shows that many residents own mobile phones and televisions in their shacks and have overcome a lack of infrastructure by rigging up elaborate – mostly illegal – electricity supplies. [...] Nationwide, more than one-third of slum homes surveyed had no indoor toilets and 64% were not connected to sewerage systems. About half of the households lived in only one room or shared with another family. However, 70% had televisions and 64% had mobile phones.

Maqbool Khan, 54, has lived in the seaside Geeta Nagar slum in South Mumbai for the last 40 years. The shantytown is close to posh apartment complexes inhabited by millionaires and senior officials. Khan runs a tailoring shop. He says that there are not enough municipal facilities for Geeta Nagar's 2,000 households. 'I feel embarrassed to tell you how we survive,' he said in a telephone interview. 'We have to queue up for hours even to go to the toilet, so we often end up doing it in the sea. The government keeps promising to shift us to proper housing, but we remain stranded here.'

'A visit to the cholera districts of Bermondsey'

The last place we went to was in Joiner's-court, with four wooden houses in it, in which there had lately been as many as five cases of cholera. In front, the poor souls, as if knowing by an instinct that plants were given to purify the atmosphere, had pulled up the paving-stones before their dwellings, and planted a few stocks here and there in the rich black mould beneath. The first house we went to, a wild ragged-headed boy shot out in answer to our knock, and putting his hands across the doorway, stood there to prevent our entrance. Our friend asked whether he could enter, and see the state of the drainage? 'No; t'ain't convenient,' was the answer, given so quickly and sharply, that the lad forced some ugly and uncharitable suspicion upon us. In the next house, the poor inmate was too glad to meet with anyone ready to sympathize with her sufferings. We were taken up to a room, where we were told she had positively lived for nine years. The window was within four feet of a high wall, at the foot of which, until very recently, ran the open common sewer. The room was so dark that it was several minutes before we could see anything within it, and there was a smell of must and dry rot that told of damp and imperfect ventilation, and the unnatural size of the pupils of the wretched woman's eyes convinced us how much too long she had dwelt in this gloomy place.

Activity 3 continued

b. Now use the skills that you have developed throughout this section to complete the exam-style question below. Begin your answer below and continue on separate paper if necessary.

> Both of these texts are about poor living conditions. Compare the following:
> - the writer's attitudes to poor living conditions
> - how the writers get across their views to the reader.   **[10]**

Support

a. Swap your work with a partner and read the assessment criteria below. Try to see which of these descriptors best fits your partner's work.

Marks	Criteria
0	Nothing worthy of credit
1–2	Identifies basic similarities and/or differences
3–4	Identifies and gives a straightforward description of some of the main similarities and differences
5–6	Identifies similarities and differences and makes some comparisons, commenting on how they are conveyed
7–8	Makes detailed comparisons, with valid comments on how they are conveyed
9–10	Makes comparisons that are sustained and detailed, showing clear understanding of how they are conveyed.

b. Write down three tips that will help your partner to improve their response to this type of question.

Activity 3 continued ------

Unit 4: Assessment Objective 4

8 Evaluating texts critically with supporting textual evidence

Learning focus:

- Revising how to evaluate texts
- Exploring techniques to use when giving a personal response

When asked to evaluate a text, you are being asked to make a judgement of something. You need to consider your opinion of the text and the effect it has on you.

✏ Activity 1

a. Look at the advertisement for Hutchins' Infallible **Corn** Remedy below carefully.

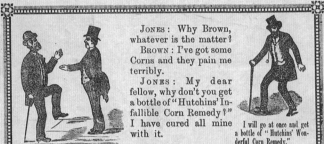

Corn: a small, painful, raised bump on the outer layer of skin.

Activity 1 continued

b. Now answer the following questions to help you evaluate the advertisement.

1. What is the text advertising?

   ----

2. Why does the writer include the conservation and cartoon drawings at the top of the page? How do they try to make you buy the ointment?

   ----

3. Look at the paragraph below the bold ONE. Pick out words and phrases that have been included to appeal to you. Do they work?

   ----

4. Look at the clever use of the bold 'ONE HUNDRED POUNDS REWARD'. Why has the writer structured the text in this way? Why is it 'clever'?

   ----

5. Look at the section 'Numerous Testimonials'. Why does the writer include this? What does it mean?

   ----

6. In the next section, beginning 'Gives ease...', what do you think about the ointment? How does the writer try to make you want to buy it?

   ----

7. Are there any other sections of the advertisement that make you wish to buy the product?

Activity 1 continued

Activity 2

Look at the mark scheme below. Use the mark scheme to help you make a checklist of what to include in your answer to an evaluation question.

Mark	Criteria
0	Nothing worthy of credit
1–2	Gives a simple personal opinion with basic textual reference
	May struggle to engage with the question
3–4	Gives a personal opinion with straightforward textual reference
	Gives some comment on the writer's views (I think she was… because…)
5–6	Gives an evaluation of the text with appropriate supporting evidence
	Some awareness of how the writer makes you feel
7–8	Gives a detailed evaluation of the text with well selected supporting evidence
	Engage with what the writer is doing and how this impacts the text
9–10	Gives a persuasive evaluation of the text with purposeful textual references
	May give perceptive overview comments
	Fully engaged with the task and text

-- ☐

-- ☐

-- ☐

-- ☐

-- ☐

My techniques for answering an evaluation question:

• Work through the text chronologically

• --

• --

• --

Activity 3

a. Read the extract below carefully.

> **'Stop swearing at the sky and join me for a snow snuggle' by India Knight**
>
> I should probably begin by extending my sympathies to anyone who is stranded in metres of snow, is low on provisions and has a boiler that's playing up, as boilers inevitably do the minute the temperature dips below zero. And I do realise that commuting is no fun if you have to drive through blizzards to get to work. And no, nobody likes sludge. [...]
>
> The newspaper headlines are already, predictably, screaming about how the country's at a standstill, we're all marooned, nothing is working, how it's an absolute disgrace that a little snow flurry shuts everything down, [...] The suggestion seems to be that things have come to such a dire pass that we'll start eating each other any second now, roaming the streets looking for small, fat people to snack on.
>
> I don't care. It's snowing! This beautiful, magical snow that transforms even the ugliest urban landscape and makes everybody feel about five years old in the best way imaginable. Snow that has the power — still, all these years later — to make fully grown men and women glue their noses to the window waiting — and then whooping when it starts. Snow is like a blanket of loveliness that concentrates the mind on what matters (fun) and what doesn't (running about for the sake of it).
>
> As I type — with an incipient cricked neck due to craning towards the window every two minutes for snow monitoring [...] my spirits soar — yes, soar — with every centimetre that piles up. My children — even the 20-year-old — are ridiculously excited because there still isn't a computer game that beats the thrill of the first snowball fight of winter.
>
> I know some people don't like it. I understand that it's no fun for the elderly — although one of the things I like so much about snow is that it engenders community spirit [...]: it's not hard to go and grit your neighbour's front steps if you're doing your own (and even if you aren't), or to knock on the door and ask if they need anything from the shops.

b. Now look at the task below and annotate it to show you understand what you are being asked to do.

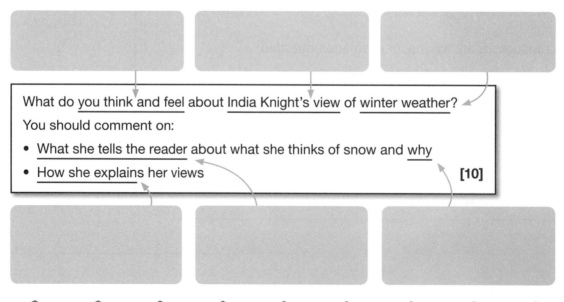

What do you think and feel about India Knight's view of winter weather?

You should comment on:

- What she tells the reader about what she thinks of snow and why
- How she explains her views   **[10]**

Activity 3 continued

c. Start preparing for this answer by reading the text and highlighting any words and phrases that suggest what the writer's view is.

d. In no more than 50 words, write a brief summary of the writer's view on winter weather. Remember to comment if she changes her view or has more than one view.

_____

_____

_____

_____

_____

e. Now complete the table below to help you prepare an answer. You will need to add some evidence of your own.

What the writer thinks of snow and why	Evidence to support this	How she explains her views
She acknowledges it can be a problem	And no, nobody likes sludge.	She selects something that most other people will dislike.
	The newspaper headlines are already, predictably, screaming about how the country's at a standstill	She stereotypes the media and ridicules them for over-reacting.
She adores snow	I don't care. It's snowing!	By dismissing the previous arguments.

Tips

- You may not need to go through all three steps each time. Sometimes the evidence selected will support your point.
- Remember to keep explanations to a minimum to allow you to cover as much of the text as possible.

107

Activity 4

10 minutes

Now you have the opportunity to use the skills you have developed in this chapter. Read the extract below carefully and complete the exam question that follows in timed conditions. Remember to read through the question carefully before you start. Highlight details from the text to help you.

Florence Nightingale's letter to *The Times* on 'Trained Nurses for the Sick Poor'

The beginning has been made, the first crusade has been fought and won, to bring [...] real nursing, trained nursing [...] to the bedsides of cases wanting real nursing among the London sick poor, in the only way in which real nurses can be so brought to the sick poor, and this by providing a real home within reach of their work for the nurses to live in—a home which gives what real family homes are supposed to give:—materially, a bedroom for each, dining and sitting rooms in common, all meals prepared and eaten in the home; morally, direction, support, sympathy in a common work, further training and instruction in it, proper rest and recreation, and a head of the home, who is also and pre-eminently trained and skilled head of the nursing [...]

[N]ursing requires the most undivided attention of anything I know, and all the health and strength both of mind and body [...] The very thing that we find in these poor sick is that they lose the feeling of what it is to be clean. The district nurse has to show them their room clean for once—in other words, to do it herself; to sweep and dust away, to empty and wash out all the appalling dirt and foulness; to air and disinfect; rub the windows, sweep the fireplace, carry out and shake the bits of old sacking and carpet, and lay them down again; fetch fresh water and fill the kettle; wash the patient and the children, and make the bed. Every home she has thus cleaned has always been kept so. She found it a pigsty, she left it a tidy, airy room.

[...] In another case, the mother had been two years in bed. The place was a den of foulness. One could cut the air with a knife. The nurse employed two of the little children to collect the foul litter and dirty linen from under the bed and sort it, emptied utensils which had not been emptied for a fortnight (this is common), cleaned the grate, and carried away the caked ashes, washed the children, combed and cleansed their hair, crowded with vermin. Next day the eldest girl, of eight, had scoured the place, and, perched on a three-legged stool, was trying to wash the dirty linen with her poor little thin arms.

What do you think and feel about Florence Nightingale's views on nursing?

You should comment on:

• what she tells readers about what nurses need and what they need to do

• how she explains her views   **[10]**

Activity 4 continued

Activity 5

Now read the student answers on the next page and then complete the following tasks.

a. Rank the responses from 1–3 in the box next to each answer (1 being the top answer and 3 the lowest).

b. Read back through the assessment criteria for an evaluation question (page 105). Try to match each answer with the appropriate section of the assessment criteria and write the numbers for this band in the box under the answer.

c. None of the answers reached the 9–10 Band. Write down two reasons why you think this is the case.

----

d. Under each of the answers, write down two things that the student needs to do to improve their answer.

Activity 5 continued

Student answer 1 ☐

Florence Nightingale is perhaps the most famous nurse in the world and when you read through this article I think her advice is straightforward and sensible. She argues that a nurse requires appropriate housing to allow her to give her 'undivided attention' to her patients. The household cleaning that a nurse is required to do shocks the reader as we don't think of these as nursing tasks – 'fetch fresh water and fill the kettle'. After she has explained her views we realize the success of the nursing as the 8-year-old girl has learned from Florence and is now able to clean the house herself.

Band: ☐

Needs to improve:

• _____

• _____

Student answer 2 ☐

I think that Florence Nightingale realizes what a vital role nurses play. She tells us that they need a 'real home' to allow nurses to give their 'most undivided attention'. Her explanations are authoritative and give the reader little room to disagree. She makes the profession sound of the utmost importance, 'Nursing requires the most undivided attention of anything I know, and all the health and strength both of mind and body', to persuade the reader that their living conditions must be suitable to give them the strength required for the post. She is realistic about what the sick need, 'they lose the feeling of what it is to be clean', and sensibly argues it is the duty of the nurse to 'show them their room clean for once'. I think the advice, which is normal today, must have been revolutionary at the time – 'empty and wash out all the appalling dirt and foulness; to air and disinfect'. I think that Nightingale argues that nursing is all about consistency, 'Every home she has thus cleaned has always been kept so.' She tells us that nurses become educators with the example of the little girl who 'had scoured the place'. Overall, I think that Florence Nightingale's views on nursing are practical, explained in a level-headed way, and relatively easy to achieve, but when they were written they must have been seen as radical and ground-breaking.

Band: ☐

Needs to improve:

• _____

• _____

Activity 5 continued

Student answer 3 ☐

Florence Nightingale was a famous nurse and I think that the comments here show to a reader why she is so famous. I think her advice was instrumental in shaping the modern nurse. Not only did she change the future of nursing but much of the advice that she gives in this article is valid today.

Band: [   ]

Needs to improve:

• --

• --

Progress check

Look back at your answer to Activity 4 on pages 108-109. Award yourself a mark by ticking one of the boxes in the table below.

Mark	Features of answer	My mark
0	Nothing worthy of credit	
1-2	Gives a simple personal opinion with basic textual reference May struggle to engage with the question	
3-4	Gives a personal opinion with straightforward textual reference Gives some comment on the writer's view ('I think she was… because…')	
5-6	Gives an evaluation of the text with appropriate supporting evidence Some awareness of how the writer makes you feel	
7-8	Gives a detailed evaluation of the text with well selected supporting evidence Engaged with what the writer is doing and how this impacts the text	
9-10	Gives a persuasive evaluation of the text with purposeful textual references May give perceptive overview comments Fully engaged with the task and text	

Component 2 Section B: Writing

Summary of Component 2 Section B: Writing

Component 2: Whole paper
• 60% of total marks for GCSE English Language
• Assessment length: 2 hours
• Section A – Reading
• Section B – Writing

Section B
• Half marks for Paper (30% of total grade)
• Complete TWO writing responses
• Time required: 1 hour (30 minutes for each question: 5 minutes' planning and 25 minutes' writing)

Section B of Component 2 tests you on the quality of your writing skills. You need to think about the purpose and audience for your writing and should aim to write about 300–400 words for each question.

Section B is worth half of the marks available for Component 2 and will be marked out of a total of 40 marks. 24 of the marks are awarded for how well you communicate and organize your ideas. The other 16 marks are available for effective vocabulary choices, controlling and varying sentence structure, accurate spelling and punctuation.

Assessment Objectives

Section B (Writing) of the Component 2 exam will test your abilities in the following assessment objectives (AOs):

AO5	Communicate clearly, effectively and imaginatively, selecting and adapting tone, style and register for different forms, purposes and audiences.
	Organize information and ideas, using structural and grammatical features to support coherence and cohesion of texts.
AO6	Use a range of vocabulary and sentence structure for clarity, purpose and effect, with accurate spelling and punctuation.

1 Formal Letters

Learning focus:

- Exploring the importance of planning and ways it can assist writing
- Drafting an effective opening to a formal letter which makes the viewpoint clear
- Developing paragraphs and a strong ending

In this lesson you will be guided through a number of activities which will help you revise how to write a formal letter. In an exam you can be asked to write to a number of different audiences for a number of different purposes.

Activity 1

a. Read the following sample exam style tasks:

1.
> Write a letter to your local MP persuading them that greater government funding is needed to support the social needs of young people in your area.

2.
> You read this part of a letter in the newspaper:
>
> > I can't believe that some people try to argue that zoos are a great step forward for the livelihood of endangered animals. This is just an excuse to overlook the cramped and unhealthy conditions they are kept in.
>
> You decide to give your views on zoos. Write the letter you would send to the editor.

3.
> Write a letter to your local MP persuading them that greater government funding is needed to support the social needs of young people in your area.

b. Now fill in the grid below to show:

- who each of the letters in the sample exam style tasks are aimed at – this is known as the **audience**
- Why the letter has been written – this is known as the **purpose**

Sample exam style task	Audience	Purpose(s)
1		
2		
3		

Activity 2

Lots of students start their answer without planning their writing. Look at these critical comments a teacher gave to their students. All of them could be helped by planning. Match up the comments to the reason for planning. The first is done for you.

Reasons for planning

1. Think of/gather ideas ——————

2. Develop your ideas with examples/detail

3. Decide on your own view before you start writing

4. Work out the most effective ideas to argue your case

5. Decide on the order of your ideas

Teacher comments

a. There is little range of ideas, more would have helped.

b. The order is muddled and there is repetition in places.

c. There is only really a topic sentence for each idea and no detail.

d. Some of the ideas do not help your argument.

e. Your viewpoint does not come across clearly as you change your mind half way through the letter.

Read the following sample exam style question:

You see this notice on the wall in school written from your Headteacher, Mrs Burnley:

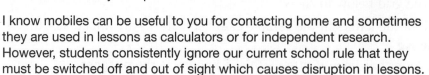

NOTICE

I am considering banning mobile phones from school and would like to hear your opinions on the matter.

I know mobiles can be useful to you for contacting home and sometimes they are used in lessons as calculators or for independent research. However, students consistently ignore our current school rule that they must be switched off and out of sight which causes disruption in lessons.

Please write a letter saying whether you think I should ban mobile phones or not. Hand your letters into the main office and I will consider your views before I make my decision.

Regards,

Mrs Burnley

Write a letter to answer her request.

Activities 3 to 9 that follow will help you write a response to the above task.

Activity 3

Work through the preparation tasks below before you start to plan your letter.

a. Highlight or annotate the purpose and audience in the task above.

b. Decide what style and format your writing will need to take (formal or informal) to be appropriate for the audience.

c. Decide what the letter needs to be about.

d. Find reasons in the letter which are for or against the topic.

Sometimes there are reasons for and against given to you in an exam task. For example, these might be for and against allowing mobile phones in school, or the reasons for or against zoos. You can use these as a starting point for your own ideas as you plan.

Activity 4

A table can be an effective planning method to see whether the reasons for or against are strongest and therefore help you decide your view. Complete the table which follows. Give your own additional ideas and, where possible, add further examples or details to the five arguments below.

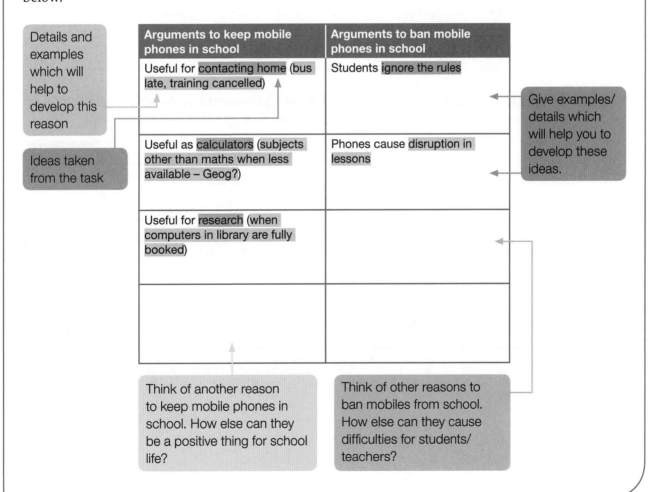

Details and examples which will help to develop this reason

Ideas taken from the task

Arguments to keep mobile phones in school	Arguments to ban mobile phones in school
Useful for contacting home (bus late, training cancelled)	Students ignore the rules
Useful as calculators (subjects other than maths when less available – Geog?)	Phones cause disruption in lessons
Useful for research (when computers in library are fully booked)	

Give examples/details which will help you to develop these ideas.

Think of another reason to keep mobile phones in school. How else can they be a positive thing for school life?

Think of other reasons to ban mobiles from school. How else can they cause difficulties for students/teachers?

Activity 5

a. Look at your arguments in Activity 4. Answer the following questions by circling **KEEP** or **BAN**:

   1. Which side has the most reasons? **KEEP / BAN**

   2. Which are your strongest reasons (the ones most likely to persuade your Headteacher)? **KEEP / BAN**

   3. Which side do you feel most strongly about? **KEEP / BAN**

b. Now write a line which states what viewpoint you are going to take in your writing:

   I am going to argue that _____

   _____

Activity 6

a. Rearrange the word tiles below to make a sentence which says what a letter opening should do. Write your answer on the line that follows.

   | opening | make | viewpoint | A | to | clear. | letter | needs | the |

   A _____.

b. Read the opening paragraphs 1-4 below. Rank order them according to which best and least follows the guidance in the sentence you wrote, A = best and D = least.

		Rank order
1.	I am writing to you to say my honest opinion of what I think about mobile phones in lessons. There are good and bad sides to this topic so I will go over them in depth.	
2.	I am writing to you because I think it is a good idea that mobile phones should be allowed in school. My view as a student should be considered. Overall, I think that mobile phones should not be allowed in school.	
3.	I am writing to you on whether we should be allowed mobile phones. In my opinion, I think we should be allowed to use our mobile phones.	
4.	I recently read your notice suggesting that there was a possibility that mobile phones could be banned from school. I wholly agree with this proposal due to the unnecessary disruption to learning that phones cause.	

Activity 6 continued

c. Read the following comments. Match them to the student's work which they best describe.

Comments	Student example 1, 2, 3 or 4
The viewpoint changes within the paragraph.	
There is a viewpoint given but it needs some ideas/details to make it more convincing.	
The topic is clear but there is no viewpoint given.	
There is a clear and convincing viewpoint which is supported by a key reason.	

d. Now write your own introduction to the task (on page 114). Make your viewpoint clear and convincing.

Activity 7

Look back at your table of planning ideas in Activity 4. Follow the tips below to help you number them to show the order they will come:

• Your first reason needs to be one which you think is really strong and convincing. Write a number 1 next to it.

• Next see if there are any paired or counter arguments. For example, an argument about mobile phones disrupting learning could be knocked down with an argument which says they assist learning when used as quick spell checkers. Remember that you need to stick to one viewpoint but that knocking the other side of the argument down can make your view stronger. You might like to show that these arguments are connected by linking them with arrows or colours on your plan.

• Finally, see if there is a logical order to any of the remaining ideas. Do they link together by topic? Number them so that they follow each other.

As you are asked to give your views, you need to make sure that what you believe comes across strongly. This will help to convince your recipient (the reader of your letter) that they should believe you or act in the way you've requested.

Activity 8

a. Read the following extract from a student's response:

> **Student answer**
>
> It is not only true to say that phones can be disruptive to learning but they can also pose a threat to students' safety. My friend was bullied because people took pictures of her getting changed in PE on their phone and then put them on the internet. Therefore, I think you should ban phones to protect students' privacy.

b. Now use this list as a guide to evaluate the student's writing:

1. Tick things which strengthen the argument. Describe the techniques being used.

2. Underline things which weaken the argument.

3. Then re-write the paragraph, removing or improving the parts which you've said weaken the argument.

4. Once you've finished writing, pass your new version to a friend. They should evaluate it for you, annotating it for parts which strengthen (i) or weaken (ii) the argument using relevant techniques or comments of their own.

5. When you've received their annotations and comments back, write a second draft to improve any parts which they thought weakened your argument.

c. Write your own improved version of the student's response:

Activity 9

a. Complete these golden rules of effective endings by adding in the missing vowels:

1. S—y s—m—th—ng wh—ch l——v—s y——r r——d—r w—nt—ng t— b—l——v— y——.

2. D—n't —sk —n —d—t—r t— wr—t— b—ck t— y——.

3. B— —ss—rt—ve b—t n—t r—d—.

b. Look at the examples of endings in the table below. They have all been written to close the letter to Mrs Burnley. Read them carefully and say whether you think they follow or break the three rules above.

Example		Which rule(s)?	Follow or breaks rule?
1.	I only know that mobile phones have been a nightmare in my school and that's the truth.		
2.	You must be an idiot if you can't see that the next generation need to embrace technology.		
3.	I feel really passionately that mobile phones should be banned from school in order that the school does its duty to protect our learning environment.		

Activity 10

Now spend 20 minutes completing your letter in full. Pay particular attention to:

- your formatting (two addresses, Dear Mrs Burnley, Yours sincerely)
- making your viewpoint clear
- developing your ideas
- keeping the tone formal for your audience.

Stretch

Angle your writing to appeal to your Headteacher by including ideas which are likely to support your case such as improving student behaviour and welfare, or exam results.

_____

_____

_____

_____

_____

_____

Activity 10 continued

Progress check

When you have received feedback from your teacher complete the work review below. List two good things about your writing ('Point 1' and 'Point 2') and one thing you need to keep in mind to help you in the final exam ('Remember'):

Point 1: _____

_____

_____

Point 2: _____

_____

_____

Remember: _____

_____

_____

For further practise on writing formal letters, choose a different task from Activity 1 on page 113 and then repeat the activities which encourage you to reflect on and check your own preparation, planning, opening, development and ending. For the letter to the MP, a spider diagram is a better planning format as you are persuading rather than arguing for or against a view.

Tip

- A formal letter includes your address top right and the recipient's address slightly below yours and on the left. You should also write the date underneath your address

- Remember the importance of making your ideas clear using appropriate punctuation and starting a new paragraph for every new reason.

2 Writing an informal letter or email

Learning focus:

- Planning and writing an informal letter or email
- Building a **rapport** with your audience

An informal letter is likely to be written to someone you know. This means that your writing style can be chattier and that you should show the kind of relationship you have with this person through your writing. The activities that follow will help you revise how to do this.

 Activity 1

The format of an informal letter differs from a formal one. Showing you know this proves to the examiner that you've considered what kind of format is necessary for the audience given in the task.

a. Look at the list of features in the table below. Decide whether they belong in an informal or formal letter, or both. Put a tick in the correct column.

Feature	Formal letter	Informal letter	Both
Addresses of both sender and receiver			
Sender's address only, or even just part of it			
Date			
Dear Sir/Madam			
Dear Mr Price (using title like Mr or Mrs)			
Dear Rachael, (using first name)			
Clear and interesting opening paragraph			
Summary			
Call to action			
Arrangements to meet or contact again			
Yours faithfully/sincerely,			
Sender's full name			
Sender's first name only			

b. Clearly, you would not end an informal letter with 'Yours faithfully' or 'Yours sincerely'. You might say something like 'See you soon' and then write your first name only. Give two other ways of closing an informal letter below:

Activity 2

This activity will help you plan an informal letter in response to this sample task:

> One of your friends is considering taking part in the talent show their school holds at the end of each year. Write an email to them, giving your view on whether they should take part. **[20]**

a. Have a look at the sample exam task above. The first thing you need to do is have a clear idea of who your audience will be. Decide on a friend that might consider doing a school talent show and write their name on the line below:

----

b. Add your own ideas to the spider diagram below. Remember that the purpose of your email is to give your view, so gathering your ideas will help you decide what you think.

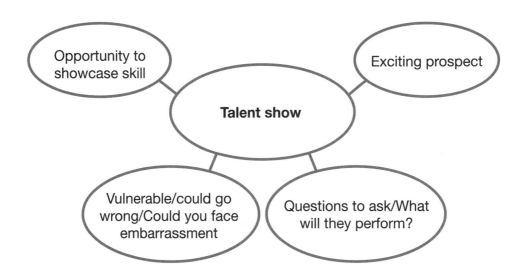

c. Now decide on the view you will take in your letter. Choose whichever view you think will be most convincing. Tick one of following options:

- Definitely don't do it! ☐
- It's up to you. ☐
- Go for it! ☐

Activity 3

Using informal language is part of getting the tone right for your audience. It does not mean your writing becomes sloppy, casual or unplanned; you should pick words and phrases that reflect a close or friendly relationship.

a. Look at the lines below. Two of them use the correct level of formality for a friend and two of them sound too formal. Decide which by ticking the appropriate box.

	Too formal	Appropriate for a friend
I think you are bonkers! Why on earth would you even consider it?		
It has been suggested by psychologists that taking risks helps young people grow.		
This sounds like a great plan, Ryan. You'll be awesome!		
It is true to say that the end of year performance is an opportunity. However, I believe it is risky strategy for someone as shy as yourself.		

b. Now have a go at rewriting the two overly formal examples into a more friendly register. Use the starting structure below for support:

- I was reading in my magazine the other day that psychologists say _____

_____

_____

- Sure, an end of year performance is an opportunity but _____

_____

_____

c. Share your work with a friend to evaluate the language choices you made. Make sure the language is now appropriate for a friend.

d. Write down one good reason why you need to make sure your language is informal when writing to a friend:

_____

_____

_____

✎ Activity 4

Building a rapport with your audience is another key skill of writing an informal letter.

a. Read the response below that was written to answer the exam-style question in Activity 2 on page 122.

> Abbie, I think this performance would be great to build your confidence. Do you remember when you sang that Florence and the Machine song last year in the karaoke we had for Simon's birthday? You were astoundingly good, hon. I was almost in tears with pride. Would you channel Flo power again do you think or go for something different to mix it up?

b. How well do you think the writer shows they know the audience?

Not at all   Partly   Really well

c. The example writing above builds a rapport with the audience by using the following features:
1. knowledge of the audience's personality
2. shared tastes, views or friends
3. past events
4. personal information about the writer
5. shared personal pronouns (we, our) and nicknames.

Find examples of these features in the response. Use colour coding or numbers to help you annotate it.

Activity 5

a. Now write an email of your own in response to the task in Activity 2. Use some of these features in Activity 4 to build the relationship with your audience.

----

b. When you have finished, give your writing to your partner or evaluate yourself how many of the features you've used successfully.

- Knowledge of the audience's personality ☐
- Shared tastes, views or friends ☐
- Past events ☐
- Personal information about the writer ☐
- Shared personal pronouns (we, our) and nicknames ☐

Activity 6

30 minutes

Use the skills you have been working on for writing informal letters and emails to write an answer to a different sample exam task:

> A younger relative of yours is about to start secondary school. Write them a letter giving advice about how to be happy and successful in their new school. **[20]**

You should spend at least 5 minutes planning your work. You have 30 minutes in total. Remember to leave some time to check your spelling and punctuation and that your ideas are clearly expressed. Write your answer on separate paper.

Progress check

When you have received feedback from your teacher, complete the work review below.

Skill being tested	I am working to achieve this skill	I have achieved this skill in places	I'm confident I've achieved this skill
Formatting informal letter			
Using a helpful planning method			
Using informal language			
Building a rapport			

Tips

- Annotate the exam task to check you know who you are writing to (audience), why you are writing (purpose), what your writing is about (topic) and the format of the writing.
- When you are planning your letter, make sure you address both sections of the task. You might do this with two bullet spider diagrams: happy and successful.
- Choose how you order your ideas carefully.
- Make sure every paragraph starts with a **topic sentence** that makes it clear what that paragraph will be about.
- Develop each paragraph with specific details.
- Make sure you choose language that is appropriate for the reader and build a rapport with your audience.

Key term

Topic sentence: often the first sentence in a paragraph, it tells the reader what the paragraph is about and is followed by other sentences which give more detail

3 Writing speeches/talks

Learning focus:

- Planning and writing a speech appropriate for audience and purpose
- Appealing to the audience by varying sentence structure

We all know that speeches/talks are intended to be listened to rather than read. But there are other things that mark them out as different from written forms of writing. You will need to keep these things in mind if you are asked to write a speech/talk as an exam task.

Activity 1

To help you understand how speeches/talks are different from writing look at the statements below. Two of these statements are true and two are false. Place a tick in the correct box for each one.

	True	False
Speeches are fixed in time and place so can use words like 'today' and 'here'.		
Speeches can be more interactive than a letter/article as the audience is present.		
Speeches are only ever to persuade you about something.		
Only speeches can adopt a point of view.		

Speeches can be for many purposes – to advise, inform, explain, argue a view, persuade, entertain – and you have already seen that letters as well as speeches can adopt a point of view. One of the things that can make a speech a special kind of form is that the speaker has a direct line to their audience. The speaker and the audience are sharing the same room and so the speaker's experiences can be brought to life in front of the audience with pictures, props or video clips. Remember that in an English exam, you are not being tested on creating a slideshow. You need to see this task as writing a script for the words that you will say. Your language choices need to show you understand that a speech is an immediate and live form.

Activity 2

Planning a speech in a way that will help you to generate and organize ideas is very important.

a. Read the sample exam task carefully.

> Your school governors have been given a grant of £1,000 from a local business to improve the social spaces for students in the school – outside or inside. Write a speech to give to your school's governors to advise them on the best way/s to spend this money.

b. Why might a list be a good way to plan for this task?

----

c. Now make a list of things you would like to see improved in your school or college's social areas. Continue the lists that have been started for you:

Inside	Outside
Water coolers	Benches
Paint	Shade/shelter

d. Now consider your own list of ideas and choose ideas that are convincing. Which ideas are likely to achieve support from the school governors? Circle them in your table above.

Tip

Choose either one main thing that has lots of different features which all the money could be spent on, or choose no more than three main ideas. That way you can use each feature of the larger item or each separate item as your topic sentence.

Support

The school governors are a group that helps to make decisions about running a school. Which of the improvements on your list might help to bring changes a governor might want to support?

Activity 3

The opening of your speech needs to:

- get the attention of your audience
- introduce who you are
- summarize your main view or idea (so for this task you should say what item or items you think the money should be spent on).

Write a short opening for your speech below including these three main features.

Activity 4

To make the ideas in your speech stand out you need to give reasons why they would be good things for the school to spend money on. You can do this by giving examples of what can happen if your chosen improvements are made. For example:

> If benches are bought then students can sit in comfort at break and lunch times instead of leaning against walls or sitting on the (often wet) grass.

List your three chosen items below. For each item think of a benefit to the school and/or pupils.

Item	Benefit

When you are writing to advise or propose ideas you will need to use **modal verbs** like 'could', 'should' and 'would'. You need to make sure you choose the right one as they have different functions:

- Could – possibility
- Should – duty/obligation
- Would – certainty

Activity 5

Look at the sample paragraph below. Practise your use of the verbs 'could', 'should' and 'would' by circling the correct one in each example. (In this paragraph, each of the verbs is only used once.)

I think you could/should/would spend the money on decent watercoolers for inside school. These could/should/would allow students to keep hydrated which we all know aids concentration. We could/should/would even begin to enjoy drinking refreshingly cooled water rather than feeling forced to buy a can from the shop at break in summer.

Activity 6

a. Read the sample response below.

Student answer

Do you remember your school yard in the summer months? The blistering heat and nowhere to hide from it...? Well, spending the whole of the £1,000 grant on a shelter might seem extravagant but it would solve the problem that so many of us face on a hot summer afternoon – lethargy. Providing us with somewhere cool would not only protect us from possible sunburn but also keep our brains more attuned to school matters and ready for afternoon learning. You see, at the moment we're forced to sit out (in what the teachers call 'the beautiful sunshine') and when we come in for class all we want to do is sleep.

b. The student answer uses 'appropriate and effective variation' of sentence structure that is 'controlled and accurate'. The student has used the following features to help achieve this variety:

1. questions or commands
2. repeated sentence forms or phrases
3. a variety of sentence lengths: e.g. a short blunt sentence next to a longer one

Activity 6 continued

4. ellipsis to indicate further unsaid ideas/a continuing list

5. dash to add extra short phrases

6. asides/parenthesis

Find examples of these features in the student's work by colour coding or annotating using the numbers 1–6.

Stretch

Which do you think is the most effective line here? Why have you chosen it?

c. Now try to use these features to appeal to your audience. Write up a paragraph from your own plan.

The end of a speech needs to leave the listening audience with a clear sense of your message, information or intentions. Often a speech can end with a 'call to action', which is a plea or order to do something.

Your ending for the exam-style question should:

• give a clear message about what the money should be spent on
• summarise why that is the best option
• thank the governors for their time
• invite them to ask you any questions about your proposal.

Activity 7

a. Write an appropriate ending paragraph for your own speech below.

---

b. Now evaluate whether you have included the four features of endings listed above. Circle them in your paragraph, and amend your ending to include any you have left out.

Activity 8

30 minutes

Now you can put together what you have learned by answering a full exam-style question.

a. Read the question below carefully.

> A free end-of-term film night with drinks and popcorn is to be held in your school hall. Your head of year has asked for students to make speeches in assembly promoting their favourite film. The students will vote to decide which films will be watched.
>
> Write the speech you would give to promote the film you would like to watch. **[20]**

b. Annotate the exam-style question to find the purpose, audience and topic for this speech.

c. Notice that the audience for this question requires a more informal style than the previous exam-style question on page 113. Look back at the work on informal language on page 123.

d. You have 30 minutes to complete your writing. Remember this time is for thinking about and ordering ideas, writing up and checking your work.

Activity 8 continued

Progress check

When you have received feedback from your teacher, complete the work review below.

Skill being tested	I am working to achieve this skill	I have achieved this skill in places	I'm confident I've achieved this skill
Recognizing differences between written and spoken formats, e.g. letter and speech			
Using a helpful planning method			
Writing an opening that gains attention, introduces the speaker and summarizes the main view			
Developing ideas with reasons and examples.			
Using the verbs 'could', 'should' and 'would' when writing to advise			
Adapting sentence structure to appeal to the audience			
Writing a strong end			

4 Writing an article

Learning focus:

* Planning and writing an article effective for audience and purpose

Articles can be found in magazines and newspapers. They can be written for different audiences, on many different topics and for different purposes.

Activity 1

a. Rearrange the following anagrams to list the features needed for an article.

tlite _____

pciurte _____

itorndctiuon _____

tpioc snenetecs _____

cluoncison _____

b. Look at the two sample exam-style questions that follow. The first has been annotated for you but there are gaps for you to identify any other key words or bits of information that will be useful for you to notice before you plan. Add to the annotations on the first question and annotate the second question in the same way.

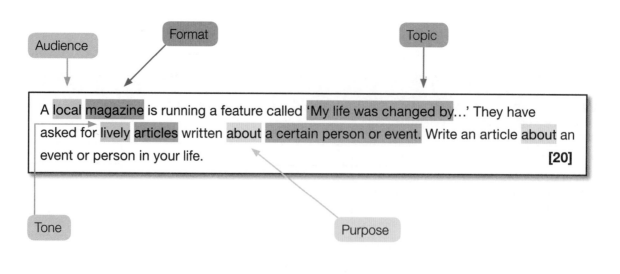

Activity 1 continued

> The issue of how ready young people are for leaving home is always coming up in the news. Write an article for your school magazine about the importance of learning life skills such as money management, cooking, road safety/driving skills. **[20]**

Activity 2

a. There are two main jobs of a headline or title. One is to give information about the topic of the article and the other is to grab the reader's attention.

    1. A reason the title or headline needs to be informative is:

    ----

    2. A reason why the title or headline needs to grab the reader's attention is:

    ----

b. When you think of a headline for your article, remember that it also needs to be appropriate for your audience. Look at the possible headlines in the table below for the first exam-style question in Activity 1. Complete the table to show how these headlines complete both jobs.

Headline	Topic of the article (informs)	How it appeals to the audience (grabs attention)
My dad: my inspiration		
My teacher taught me to dream		
Clowning around: My grandad's red nose and unicycle		

Activity 2 continued

c. Which do you think is the most effective and why?

Support

If a title was 'Hot to Shop', what would you expect the article to be about? Would you be surprised if it was about holidays? Why does the title of an article need to relate to the topic? What might happen if it doesn't?

Stretch

What techniques can you identify in the titles/headlines given in the table above?

d. Now write three possible headlines for the second exam-style question from Activity 1. Remember to try to use some techniques to appeal to your reader. You might include a pun (play on words), direct appeal, question, shock tactic, alliteration, rhyme, repetition or other things you can think of, but try not to overdo it!

Activity 3

a. As with all writing tasks, you need to plan your writing. Fill in the gaps with the missing vowels to complete the reasons for planning:

1. I need to work out the T_P_C or V_ _W of my writing.

2. I need to gather I_E_S so I have plenty to write about.

3. I need to think of D_T_I_S and E_ _M P_ _ S to help me develop my ideas.

4. I need to know how to S_ _U_T_ _E my writing so my ideas have a clear order and shape.

b. Now complete the spider diagram opposite to plan your article for your school magazine about the importance of life skills. You annotated an exam-style question on page 135 so you already know the audience (parents), topic (life skills, being ready for life out of school) and purpose (comment/argue). Try to develop each 'leg' of the spider with details.

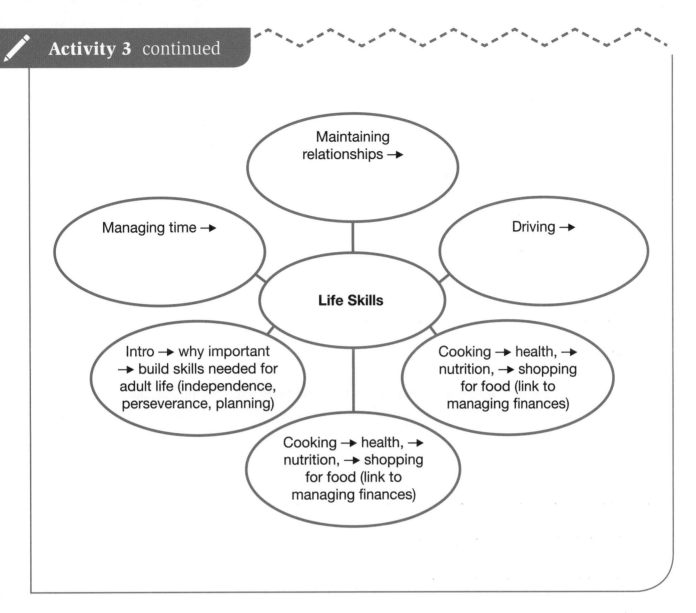

If you've planned using a spider diagram, you will already have helped yourself begin to organize your ideas. Each 'leg' of your spider will become a paragraph of your article. The main topic, which is next to the body of the spider will become the topic sentence. To plan the order of your ideas, first find ideas that link together. For example, shopping for healthy food might be linked to living on a budget, which covers both cooking and finances. You might therefore choose to order your paragraphs so that your ideas can follow on and your paragraphs link up like this:

How much money is left after bills impacts on what money is left for shopping. If students are taught skills of how to manage their budget then they will also be able to work out what ingredients they can afford to plan healthy meals...

Activity 4

a. Have a look at this article opening. It makes the topic clear and gives a reason to support the idea.

> Ms Long was my English teacher. She was my inspiration as she taught me how to aim higher. She always used to talk about interesting things that made us listen.

b. How successful is it against AO5 (communication and organization)? Evaluate it and give the student a target for improvement.

Mark: _____

Comment: _____

Target: _____

c. Now write your own opening. Remember to use ambitious and specific vocabulary, an idea or details that will grab your reader's attention and information which makes the topic clear.

_____

_____

_____

_____

_____

Activity 5

Drawing a conclusion to an article is really important as it is the last thing your audience will read.

a. In the conclusion opposite the student has thought carefully about the kind of lasting impressions they want to leave about their teacher. Read it to find these impressions.

Activity 5 continued

Student conclusion

It wasn't that she was the pint-sized powerhouse of the English department; it wasn't that she reminded us of a rock star in her end of year performance; it wasn't even that she seemed to know everything about any subject – although that was quite impressive. When she sat, perched on her desk, short legs crossed, she held us – mesmerised – with her every word. Somehow, her words were magical and transported us outside of that grotty, ramshackle school. It was because of that that she was an inspiration: she made me want to go and discover more about the topics she opened the door on.

b. Annotate the student conclusion with comments about the techniques the student has used. You might look at:

- repetition
- humour
- imagery/description
- evaluation/judgement

Activity 6

Put together what you have learnt over the last five activities to help you answer **one** of the tasks below:

Many things which were once accepted are now illegal, for example it is now illegal to smoke in a car if a person under 16 is present. In the same way, certain things are becoming more acceptable, for example the use of robots, self-driving cars, e-cigarettes. Write a lively article commenting on things which you think will become less or more acceptable in the future. **[20]**

A business magazine is running a feature called 'Work experience for 14–16 year olds: are they too immature or is it a learning opportunity not to be missed?' They want to find out the opinions of students about work experience placements. You decide to write an article giving your views.

[20]

Activity 6 continued

30 minutes

Annotate your chosen question to identify the purpose, audience, topic, tone and format. Plan your answer, order your ideas, and then write your introduction, develop your paragraphs and draw a conclusion. Remember to appeal to the audience throughout. You have 30 minutes in total. Plan your writing here and write your answer on a blank piece of paper.

Progress check

When you have received feedback from your teacher, complete the work review below.

Skill being tested	I am working to achieve this skill	I have achieved this skill in places	I'm confident I've achieved this skill
Writing a headline that informs and grabs attention			
Using a helpful planning method			
Organizing ideas and linking paragraphs			
Writing a clear opening			
Writing a conclusion which leaves a lasting impression			

5 Reports

Learning focus:

- Revise the specific structure of a report
- Plan and write a report appropriate for purpose and audience

A report is often a formal writing style written to someone in a position of authority like a head teacher, or someone whom you do not know personally, such as a business person or another adult. Its purpose is to convey information about a certain topic or brief, to identify a problem and to offer guidance on how this might be solved. The report has quite a specific structure that you need to follow.

Activity 1

The following features of a report are in the wrong order. Reorder them.

Title giving topic	1. _____
Observations/ideas, details.	2. _____
Introduction	3. _____
Actions	4. _____
Closing – thanks for reading report…	5. _____
Priorities	6. _____

Activity 2

The title of a report needs to make the subject clear.

a. Look at the report task below. Annotate the task to identify the topic of the writing and the audience.

> A research panel is looking to collect information about schools' rewards systems. They have asked for reports to be written on:
> - what kind of behaviour is rewarded and the type of rewards given;
> - any action students feel needs to be taken. [20]

Activity 2 continued

b. Now look at the three titles below. Match each of the titles to the genre (type of writing), audience(s) and topic it belongs to.

Title	Genre/Audience/Topic
Re: Strict Behaviour Systems	Research report outlining systems for rewards
Banishing Bad Behaviour	Formal letter to editor/headteacher/year leader/parents on school systems.
Report to: Research Panel concerning School Reward Systems	Article for teachers or parents on banishing bad behaviour.

Support

What clues are there in the style of writing which help you to match the titles to their genres? For example, alliteration, research panel.

Activity 3

A spider diagram is a good planning method to help you generate ideas for your report as you can add details and link ideas together.

A research panel is looking to collect information about schools' rewards systems.

They have asked for reports to be written on:

- what kind of behaviour is rewarded and the type of rewards given;
- any action students feel needs to be taken. **[20]**

For the exam-style question above, complete the spider diagram to plan your ideas.

Tip

Just remember that ideas and details you provide do not have to be true, but they should be realistic, not ridiculous. If you have got a friend in a different school whose school has rewards days and you would like to write as if that happens in your school (to give yourself more to write) then go ahead. The examiner will not know or mind! They are more interested in the way you structure, express and develop your ideas and how convincing your work is.

Activity 3 continued

letters home,
rewards days,
teacher praise

methods of
reward

Life Skills

types of
behaviour

academic
achievement,
effort, citizenship,
improvement

Remember that your introduction needs to:

- say why you are writing the report
- outline the key features of the rewards system in your school
- consider what action might be taken.

Activity 4

The introduction below does two of these three things. Tick them off as you read. Add in a sentence or two below to complete it with the missing part.

This report considers the rewards systems in place in Wharton School in Bristol. Currently, there are a number of different rewards given through the year for students' academic achievement, persistent effort and citizenship, such as postcards home and teacher praise. Then at the end of the academic year there are certificates awarded for the best overall achievement, most improved student and best effort in each subject.

In the paragraphs that follow your introduction you should develop some details about the types of behaviour rewarded and the method of reward. You could discuss whether you think they are fair or effective rewards. Remember that your writing is to identify any problems with the current system (if there are any).

Activity 5

Rewrite the paragraph below by making sure the information is relevant for the report. Add in more details about why the certificates are given, make the language formal and correct any spellings which are wrong.

> We are given certifcates at our school. My mate Joe got on the other day. I think Peter has had one too.

Activity 6

In Activity 5 you identified things that might be changed or improved. In the next section of your report you should suggest what can be done. Complete the paragraph below to help you practise:

> Our school doesn't currently have a rewards day, which I think is a real shame. I know that teaching time is precious but I don't see why those who have persistently put in the effort to make their work the best it can be can't have one day off with their friends. If this were used as a carrot for good behaviour to win those round who misbehave, then...

Activity 7

One of the key reasons for writing a report is to give recommendations about a topic or area. These can be clearly presented as a list of bullet points at the end.

To finish off your report on school rewards systems, list three main comments about the current system in your school and three ideas for improvement.

Fill in the bullet points below.

The current rewards system:

* _____

* _____

* _____

Actions/improvements:

* _____

* _____

* _____

To close your report you should thank the person reading it and sign off with your name like the example below.

Thank you for taking the time to read my report on the rewards system in place at Wharton School. I hope the information and suggestions I have provided to you will be useful for your research.

Niamh Coleman

Activity 8

30 minutes

Now have a go at completing the report task below in 30 minutes. Spend about five minutes planning. Use the structure in Activity 1 on page 141 to make sure your ideas follow the correct format. Remember to leave some time to check the accuracy of your writing and that it all makes sense to the reader. Plan your writing here and continue on separate sheets of paper.

> Students are unhappy with the current eating provision at their school and have expressed their concerns to the head teacher, who has asked them to write a formal report on the issue. The report is to include:
> - the type of existing food outlets, the food they offer and its cost
> - types of foods students might like to see on offer in the local area. **[20]**

Progress check

When you have received feedback from your teacher, complete the work review below.

Skill being tested	I am working to achieve this skill	I have achieved this skill in places	I'm confident I've achieved this skill
Choosing a clear title			
Using a spider diagram to generate ideas and details			
Writing an introduction that gives a reason for the report, key features of the topic and action to be taken			
Developing relevant details			
Recommending action by giving priorities in bullet points			
Closing report with thanks and sign-off			

6 Writing a review

Learning focus:

- Writing a review which follows an appropriate structure and gives a recommendation to the audience
- Using **parenthesis** to add in extra information and views

You might well have read reviews online or in magazines as a way of deciding whether to read a certain book, watch a particular film or go to a certain place or event. Although reviews can be written about lots of different topics, they generally share the same features.

Activity 1

Look at the clues on the right in order to fill in the crossword with the features of reviews.

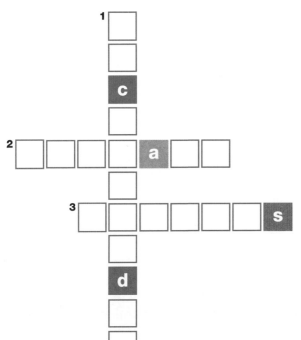
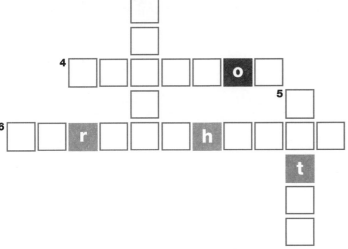

Across

2 A brief overview of the plot/place/event

3 You might gives these to explain your opinion

4 A thought/view about the thing being reviewed

6 Words (often in brackets) to show extra information or views

Down

1 Whether you would advise the person to read it/watch it/do it/see it

5 A heading that summarizes the view

Activity 2

The title to a review can just give the title of a book or film. It can also indicate the writer's viewpoint about what they are reviewing. Each of the following titles are for reviews from teenage readers of the novel *Mister Pip* by Lloyd Jones.

a. Read each title carefully and decide which review gave 1 star (terrible), 3 stars (ok) and 5 stars (amazing).

Title	Star rating
Devastatingly beautiful narrative	
A loveable narrator but too brutal a plot	
A trudge of a read through unnecessary details	

b. Circle the words in each title that told you the opinion of the reviewer.

c. Choose a novel or video game that you might review for a teenage audience. Write a title that gives your opinion of it. Have in mind your star recommendation but do not write it down.

Title

----

d. Now show your title to someone else. Can they guess your star rating?

Activity 3

A summary gives the main points. It allows the reader to get a background to the film or an outline of the plot so that they understand some of the reasons behind the opinions given.

a. Read the summary paragraph below that opens a review of a local fish and chip shop. List five pieces of factual information given about the shop.

> Rock and Sole is a delightful little coastal chippy on High Beach in South Devon. It offers traditional fayre at a good price and, for a place barely bigger than a kiosk, must serve a few thousands of tourists each day.

Factual information given:

- --
- --
- --
- --
- --

Activity 4

a. Now practise writing a summary of the novel or computer game you chose in Activity 2. You might like to create a table like this to help you pick out key features.

Title and author/ creator of game/ novel	Character(s)	Story or aim of game/key events in novel	Genre of game/ novel	Other game/novels by same creator/writer you might have played/read

----

Activity 5

Review texts use parenthesis to give extra information and opinions. This extra information might be shown between brackets or dashes. In the restaurant review on the next page, the punctuation has been left in to suggest where you might add in information or your view.

Activity 5 continued

Fill in the gaps with ideas, details or personal comments that you think might fit here.

I chose the carbonara pizza (_____

_____) which was more oily than usual. My egg was

not runny as requested (_____

_____) and the pancetta was likewise not sensitively cooked

(_____).

Stretch

Try to make your insertions lively to build the relationship with the reader.

Support

If you're struggling for what might go in each space, have a look at the following examples and try versions of your own:

- a regular choice for me
- in fact it was so solid it looked like a large boil on my pizza
- it was so burnt I couldn't stomach it

Activity 6

Everyone expects a recommendation at the end of a review – it is one of the reasons that we read them. Your recommendation can:

- give strong approval

> A worthy contender for your money. I'd say you should go the next opportunity you get.

- recommend, but with conditions

> If you can stand the terrible décor, the food is very good value and the chefs are inventive. It's well worth a try.

- or advise against

> In short, I wouldn't bother. You'd be better off in the pub up the road where the hygiene standards are higher and the food is freshly prepared.

Write your own recommendation for the novel or computer game you've been reviewing:

_____

_____

_____

_____

_____

30 minutes

Activity 7

Now is your chance to put your revision work into practice on an exam-style question. You have 30 minutes in total to gather and order your ideas, write and check your response. Start by annotating the task to identify the purpose, audience, format and tone. Then plan your writing below and continue on seperate sheets of paper.

> A website for young people called 'Get Out There' publishes reviews of music, drama or sporting events. Review an event which you have been to or seen on television. **[20]**

Progress check

When you have received feedback from your teacher, complete the work review below.

Skill being tested	I am working to achieve this skill	I have achieved this skill in places	I'm confident I've achieved this skill
Writing an informative title			
Summarizing in order to give lots of information in a short space			
Using parenthesis to add in extra detail			
Giving a recommendation that makes your view clear			
Giving a star rating			

Sample Component 1

Section A: 40 marks

The extract is taken from 'Raymond's Run' by Toni Cade Bambara.

I don't have much work to do around the house like some girls. My mother does that. [...] And anything else that's got to get done, my father does. All I have to do in life is mind my brother Raymond, which is enough.

Sometimes I slip and say my little brother Raymond. But as any fool can see he's much bigger and he's older too. But a lot of people call him my little brother cause he needs looking after cause he's not quite right. And a lot of smart mouths got lots to say about that too. [...] Now, if anybody has anything to say to Raymond, anything to say about his big head, they have to come by me. And I don't [...] believe in standing around with somebody in my face doing a lot of talking. I'd much rather just knock you down and take my chances even if I am a little girl with skinny arms and a squeaky voice, which is how I got the name Squeaky. And if things get too rough, I run. And as anybody can tell you, I'm the fastest thing on two feet.   5

  10

There is no track meet that I don't win the first-place medal. [...] The big kids call me Mercury cause I'm the swiftest thing in the neighborhood. Everybody knows that. [...] So as far as everyone's concerned, I'm the fastest and that goes for Gretchen, too, who has put out the tale that she is going to win the first-place medal this year. Ridiculous. In the second place, she's got short legs. In the third place, she's got freckles. In the first place, no one can beat me and that's all there is to it.   15

I'm standing on the corner admiring the weather and about to take a stroll down Broadway so I can practice my breathing exercises, and I've got Raymond walking on the inside close to the buildings. [...] Sometimes if you don't watch him he'll dash across traffic to the island in the middle of Broadway and give the pigeons a fit. Then I have to go behind him apologizing to all the old people sitting around trying to get some sun and getting all upset with the pigeons fluttering around them, scattering their newspapers and upsetting the [...] lunches in their laps. So I keep Raymond on the inside of me, and he plays like he's driving a stage coach which is OK by me so long as he doesn't run me over or interrupt my breathing exercises, which I have to do on account of I'm serious about my running, and I don't care who knows it. [...]   20

  25

So I'm strolling down Broadway breathing out and breathing in on counts of seven, which is my lucky number, and here comes Gretchen and her sidekicks: Mary Louise, who used to be a friend of mine when she first moved to Harlem from Baltimore and got beat up by everybody till I took up for her. [...] Now she hangs out with the new girl Gretchen and talks about me like a dog; and Rosie, who is as fat as I am skinny and has a big mouth where Raymond is concerned and is too stupid to know that there is not a big deal of difference between herself and Raymond and that she can't afford to throw stones. [...]   30

  35

"You signing up for the May Day races?" smiles Mary Louise, only it's not a smile at all. A dumb question like that doesn't deserve an answer. [...]

"I don't think you're going to win this time," says Rosie. [...]

"I always win cause I'm the best," I say straight at Gretchen. [...] Gretchen smiles, but it's not a smile, and I'm thinking that girls never really smile at each other because they don't   40 know how and don't want to know how and there's probably no one to teach us how, cause grown-up girls don't know either. [...]

I take my time getting to the park on May Day because the track meet is the last thing on the program. The biggest thing on the program is the May Pole dancing, which I can do without, thank you, even if my mother thinks it's a shame I don't take part and act like a girl for a change. You'd think my mother'd be grateful not to have to [...] buy me new white baby-doll shoes that can't be taken out of the box till the big day. You'd think she'd be glad her daughter ain't out there prancing around a May Pole getting [...] new clothes all dirty and sweaty and trying to act like a fairy or a flower or whatever you're supposed to be when you should be trying to be yourself, [...] which is, as far as I am concerned, a poor black girl who really can't afford to buy shoes and a new dress you only wear once a lifetime cause it won't fit next year. 45 50

I was once a strawberry in a Hansel and Gretel pageant when I was in nursery school and didn't have no better sense than to dance on tiptoe with my arms in a circle over my head doing umbrella steps and being a perfect fool just so my mother and father could come dressed up and clap. You'd think they'd know better than to encourage that kind of nonsense. I am not a strawberry. I do not dance on my toes. I run. That is what I am all about. [...] 55

I put Raymond in the little swings, which is a tight squeeze this year and will be impossible next year. [...] The man on the loudspeaker has just announced the fifty-yard dash, although he might just as well be giving a recipe for angel food cake cause you can hardly make out what he's saying for the static. I get up and slip off my sweat pants and then I see Gretchen standing at the starting line, kicking her legs out like a pro. Then as I get into place I see that [...] Raymond is [...] on the other side of the fence, bending down with his fingers on the ground just like he knew what he was doing. I was going to yell at him but then I didn't. It burns up your energy to holler. 60 65

Every time, just before I take off in a race, I always feel like I'm in a dream, the kind of dream you have when you're sick with fever and feel all hot and weightless. [...] But once I spread my fingers in the dirt and crouch over [...], the dream goes and I am solid again and am telling myself, Squeaky you must win, you must win, you are the fastest thing in the world [...]. The pistol shot explodes in my blood and I am off and weightless again, flying past the other runners, my arms pumping up and down and the whole world is quiet except for the crunch as I zoom over the gravel in the track. I glance to my left and there is no one. To the right, a blurred Gretchen. [...] And on the other side of the fence is Raymond with his arms down to his side and the palms tucked up behind him, running in his very own style, and it's the first time I ever saw that and I almost stop to watch my brother Raymond on his first run. But the white ribbon is bouncing toward me and I tear past it, racing into the distance. [...] I lean down to catch my breath and here comes Gretchen walking back, for she's overshot the finish line too, huffing and puffing with her hands on her hips taking it slow, breathing in steady time like a real pro and I sort of like her a little for the first time. [...] We both wondering just who did win. [...] 70 75 80

Then I hear Raymond yanking at the fence to call me and I wave to shush him, but he keeps rattling the fence like a gorilla in a cage [...], but then like a dancer or something he starts climbing up nice and easy but very fast. And it occurs to me, watching how smoothly he climbs [...] that Raymond would make a very fine runner. Doesn't he always keep up with me on my trots? And he surely knows how to breathe in counts of seven cause he's always doing it at the dinner table, which drives my brother George up the wall. And I'm smiling [...] cause if I've lost this race, or if me and Gretchen tied, or even if I've won, I can always retire as a runner and begin a whole new career as a coach with Raymond as my champion. After all, [...] if I bugged my mother, I could get piano lessons 85 90 and become a star. And I have a big rep as the baddest thing around. And I've got a roomful of ribbons and medals and awards. But what has Raymond got to call his own?

So I stand there with my new plans, laughing out loud by this time as Raymond jumps down from the fence and runs over. [...] The men on the loudspeaker have finally gotten themselves together and compared notes and are announcing "In first place—Miss Hazel Elizabeth Deborah Parker." (Dig that.) "In second place—Miss Gretchen P. Lewis." And I look over at Gretchen wondering what the "P" stands for. And I smile. [...] She's good, no doubt about it. Maybe she'd like to help me coach Raymond; she obviously is serious about running, as any fool can see. [...] She nods to congratulate me and then she smiles. And I smile. We stand there with this big smile of respect between us. It's about as real a smile as girls can do for each other, considering we don't practice real smiling every day, you know, cause maybe we [are] too busy being flowers or fairies or strawberries instead of something honest and worthy of respect . . . you know . . . like being people.

95

100

Toni Cade Bambara

A1 **Read lines 1–12**

List five things you learn about Squeaky. **[5 marks]**

A2 **Read lines 13–35**

How does the writer show that Squeaky is a good runner and that she takes running seriously? *You must refer to the language used in the text to support your answer* **[5 marks]**

A3 **Read lines 36–58**

What does Squeaky think and feel about activities like May Pole dancing and taking part in a school pageant? *You must refer to the language used in the text to support your answer* **[10 marks]**

A4 **Look at lines 59–81**

How does the writer convey the drama of Squeaky's race? *You must refer to the language used in the text to support your answer* **[10 marks]**

A5 **Look at lines 82–end**

"Towards the end of this passage, the writer shows some important changes in Squeaky's character" To what extent do you agree with this view? **[10 marks]**

You should write about:

• your own impressions of Squeaky and her situation as she is presented here and in the passage as a whole;

• how the writer has created these impressions.

You must refer to the text to support your answer.

Section B: 40 marks

*In this section you will be assessed for the quality of your **creative prose writing** skills.*

24 marks are awarded for communication and organisation; 16 marks are awarded for vocabulary, sentence structure, spelling and punctuation.

You should aim to write about 450–600 words.

Choose one of the following titles for your writing: **[40 marks]**

Either,   **(a)** Write about an occasion when you supported a friend

Or,   **(b)** The trap

Or,   **(c)** Write a story which begins:
Life had been good, until now.

Or,   **(d)** Write about an incident when you had to show courage

Sample Component 2

Section A: 40 marks

Two resources are required to answer the questions below. Text A is a newspaper article, 'What I learned from spending a night with the homeless' written by Adriana Colado. Text B is an extract from 'Diary of Arthur Mumby.'

Read the newspaper article, 'What I learned from spending a night with the homeless'.

A1   **(a)** Name the place where the Sleep East Fundraiser event took place.   **[1]**

      (b) Name one thing that volunteers took with them to help them get through the night.   **[1]**

      (c) Give one reason why there was sadness in Rep's eyes.   **[1]**

A2   What do you think and feel about Adriana Colado's decision to spend a night as a homeless person?   **[10]**

To answer the following questions you need to read the extract from the 'Diary of Arthur Mumby.'

A3   **(a)** Where does Arthur Mumby see the homeless people?   **[1]**

      (b) Where can the homeless people find a soup kitchen?   **[1]**

      (c) Why does Arthur Mumby think some of the women were not all from a working class background?   **[1]**

A4   **How does Arthur Mumby persuade the reader to feel pity for the homeless?** **[10]**

      To answer the following questions you will need to use both texts.

A5   Using information from both texts, explain how homeless people pass the time.   **[4]**

A6   Both of these texts are about homelessness.

Compare:

(a) How the writers feel about homeless people they see

(b) How the writers get across their views to the reader.   **[10]**

You must use the text to support your comments and make it clear which text you are referring to.

Text A

<u>What I learned from spending a night with the homeless</u>

A few days ago I decided to sleep rough for one night to raise money for homeless people.

I remember browsing my phone [...] and finding out about the Sleep Easy fundraiser event hosted by the YMCA. It challenged the reader to give up on their comfort and spend a cold winter night on the streets of Kingston. [It was suggested that I] could also set up a fundraising page and encourage others to donate. The motto was "sleep rough so others don't have to." I did not fully understand how sleeping in the cold could help anyone, but a voice in my head told me to just do it. So I did.   5

Before I arrived at the Memorial Gardens, where it took place, I did not have great expectations. [...] What I did imagine, however, was to see a lot of warm, friendly people with only several layers of clothing on and a thermal flask to get them through the night.   10

As I entered the church, I heard the sounds of ongoing speeches and performances. A young man read his story to the audience, musicians sang, spokespeople spoke, people clapped. I found myself wondering why they felt the need to entertain us before sending us outside to sleep "rough".

When we finally went outside, we were given a thermal flask and a big cardboard box to   15
sleep in. As I wandered around the garden looking for the perfect spot to settle, I observed the crowd. I realised I was among big organised school groups and a few other groups of people – but I was alone.

The teenagers were excited to spend a night with their mates and no parents around; and the adults were busy finding ways to make themselves as comfortable as possible. It all   20
felt more like camping than anything else. There were pillows, blankets, yoga mats and other things designed to make the night less painful. Inside the church there was coffee, juice and soup. Whoever was too cold to stay out could sit inside or play table tennis.

Maybe this wasn't the brightest idea, I started convincing myself. I did not know who to approach and I started feeling lonely. But then I heard two loud, husky voices behind me. I   25
looked behind me and saw two homeless people on a bench in the dark. I turned my face back, but then I looked again. I decided to join them. As soon as I sat down, I was offered a cigarette, which I accepted [...].

They were a homeless married couple whose faces carried many years of struggle. I was not shy to ask who they were and what brought them there. Their openness amazed me.   30

Rep was in his late fifties and he had short, grey hair. He told me he fought in the Falklands War, in Cyprus, as well as in Ireland. He said he got tired of fighting and decided to quit the army, but that he still carried the heavy weight of the lives he took on his shoulders. Louise was a short-haired woman full of joy and passion for music. She played the guitar and told me she loved Pearl Jam. Her favourite song was Yellow Ledbetter. I told her I did not have   35
Pearl Jam in my playlist, but I could play Foo Fighters. As I put the song on, she started singing and dancing.

While Louise enjoyed the tune, Rep opened up to me. The couple had been on the streets for as long as I have lived, which petrified me. "Aren't you tired of wandering around?", I asked. Rep said he wanted to stop, but did not know how to do it. After two decades of   40
homelessness, the idea of "normality" sounded like a **utopia**. He spoke about his family and his daughters, which he had not seen for years. I could read the sadness in his eyes as he continued.

Leaving the streets is not as easy as one might think. Rep was a soldier and fighting was his craft. When he quit the army because the burden of taking lives became heavier than his conscience could take, he did not know what else he was good at. The psychological impact that those war zones had on him was greater than [...he] would like to admit. Despite his past and his present, his integrity remained his greatest feature. 45

As the hours went by, the group got bigger and the immense respect for Rep was evident. He truly was a remarkable man – the "real deal" as they often repeated. A harsh man, but also very kind. Both of them were very popular among the homeless community, but Louise did not give much away about her deepest thoughts. She preferred to face people with a smile and positive attitude, but I knew that deep down she was a scarred woman. 50

The homeless of Kingston might not have a bed, but they have each other. All of them shared the same feeling towards the "campers" in the garden and the event itself – those people did not understand homelessness. And neither did I. I had not expected to understand it, because that would have been foolish of me. But I realised that raising "awareness" or showing solidarity towards a cause will not change anything. Spending a night with them will not either. I realised that this experience did not change their lives a single bit. But it changed mine, and that's the hypocritical side of our society. We feel awakened by this sort of experience, and we feel blessed for what we are and what we have. We are helping ourselves by trying to help others and it is a learning experience to be able to see the other side. [...] That is a remarkable thing, but one will never understand homelessness unless he is left without a roof. 55

60

After hours of hanging around Kingston and seeing life through their eyes, I left without a goodbye. I felt guilt and shame, even though it is not my fault I am privileged. I could not bring myself to say thank you or goodbye, because I had a bed and friends waiting for me at home – but they had no choice but to stay. I walked away with a bittersweet feeling. I was weak at that moment and I [...] regret it. But I will never regret turning around and sitting on that bench with them. I will take that night and their kindness with me forever. 65

70

Adriana Colado

utopia–paradise

Text B

<u>Friday, 15 July</u>

Walking through St. James's Park about 4 p.m., I found the open spaces of **sward** on either side of the path thickly dotted over with strange dark objects. They were human beings; ragged men and ragged women; lying prone and motionless, not as those who lie down for rest and enjoyment, but as creatures worn out and listless. A park keeper came up: "Who are these?" I asked. "They are men out of work," said he, "and unfortunate girls; servant girls, many of them, what has been out of a place and took to the streets, till they've sunk so low that they can't get a living. It's like this every day, till winter comes; and then what they do I don't know. They come as soon as the gates opens; always the same faces: they bring broken **victuals** with 'em, or else goes to the soup kitchen in Vinegar Yard; and except for that, they lie about here all day. It's a disgrace Sir," (said he), "to go on in a **city** like this; and foreigners to see it, too! Why **sir**, these unfortunates are all over 5

10

the place: the ground is lousy with them." I looked and looked and still they did not move. The men were more or less tattered, but their dress was working dress, & so did not seem out of place. But the girls were clothed in what had once been finery: filthy draggled muslins; thin remnants of shawls, all rent and gaping; crushed and greasy bonnets of fashionable shape, with sprigs of torn flowers, bits of faded velvet, hanging from them. Their hands and faces were dirty & weather stained; and they lay, not (as far as I saw) herding with the men, but singly or in little groups; sprawling about the grass in attitudes ungainly, and unfeminine, and bestial: one flat on her face, another curled up like a dog with her head between her knees; another with her knees bent under her, and her cheek on the ground, and her arms spread out stiff and awkward, on either side of her. Every pose expressed an absolute degradation and despair: and the silence and deadness of the prostrate crowd was appalling. I counted these as I went along; and on one side only of the path there were one hundred and five of them. One hundred and five forlorn and **foetid** outcasts – women, many of them – grovelling on the sward, in the bright sunshine of a July afternoon, with Carlton House Terrace and Westminster Abbey looking down at them, and infinite well-drest citizens passing by on the other side.

        15

        20

        25

sward–lawn

victuals–food

foetid–foul-smelling

Section B: 40 marks

Answer Question B1 and Question B2.

In this section you will be assessed on the quality of your writing skills.

For each question, 12 marks are awarded for communication and organisation; 8 marks are awarded for vocabulary, sentence structure, punctuation and spelling.

Think about the purpose and audience for your writing.

You should aim to write about 300–400 words for each task.

B1 Your school/college is keen to raise some money for homeless people. Write a report for the Headteacher/Principal suggesting ways this might be done.

You could include:
- examples of why homeless people need our support
- your ideas about how you could raise money for this. [20]

B2 Write a lively article for a teenage magazine about the impact of computer games on teenagers' lives. [20]

Glossary

Alliteration the same letter or sound at the beginning of a group of word for special effect

Analyse to examine something methodically and in detail, in order to explain and interpret it

Chronologically in the order in which things occurred

Dialogue the words spoken by people in a piece of writing

Empathy the ability to share or understand another person's feelings

Evaluate to form an idea of the state or value of something

Explicit information that is stated clearly and openly

First-person (I/we) using first-person narrative allows you to tell a story from the perspective of a character in the text

Impression effect produced on the mind, ideas

Implicit suggested but not directly expressed

Inference a conclusion reached on the basis of evidence and reasoning

Metaphor a figure of speech in which a word or phrase is used to describe an object or an action without using 'as' or 'like'

Interpret to explain the meaning of something said or written, or of someone's actions

Modal verb a verb such as 'could', 'should' or 'may' that expresses a possibility or necessity

Motivation what a character wants to get/do/achieve. Your reader needs to understand what your character wants to achieve if they are going to sympathize with them or see their point of view

Overview a general summary, explanation or outline of a situation

Parenthesis an additional word, phrase or sentence inserted into a passage that is grammatically complete without it, marked off by brackets, dashes or commas

Perspective a particular way of thinking about something

Preposition words like 'in', 'on', or 'over' that connect a noun, noun phrase or pronoun to another word

Rapport an understanding relationship between people

Scan look quickly through a text to find specific details, rather than reading it closely to take in all the information

Simile a figure of speech in which one thing is compared to another using the words 'as' or 'like'

Speech tags these indicate dialogue and tell you how the words are spoken, i.e. 'said', 'shouted', or 'whispered'

Synthesize to combine or put together

Third-person (he/she/it/they) using third-person narrative means the story is told from an independent point of view so you can see what all the characters think and feel

Topic sentence often the first sentence in a paragraph, it tells the reader what the paragraph is about and is followed by other sentences which give more detail.

Vowels the letters 'a', 'e', 'i', 'o' and 'u'